what others are saying about
saying about
THE POWER OF friendship

"Seventy-five years as lifelong friends—and counting! *The Power of Friendship* is a heartwarming memoir, which inspires us to value and nurture our own friendships to enrich our lives. As shared by two very relatable, joyful and positive-focused women, who possess infinite wisdom and a warm sense of humor, through life's joys and challenges."

Galynn Brady
Loving wife.
Mother of Tom Brady and three beautiful daughters.
Cancer survivor.

"A beautiful tale rich with warmth and compassion, two octogenarians reminisce over the experiences and wisdom gained from enjoying a 70-plus-year history of friendship. Connected since childhood and now finding themselves in life's final chapter, they discuss changing times, tragedy, secrets and—above all—hope, over a shared love of enjoying ice cream from the serenity of park benches. The story of an unyielding bond through changing times, *The Power of Friendship* inspires readers with their collective wisdom on the value of keeping God, family, and community at the center of a life well lived."

Lynda Cheldelin Fell
Creator of award-winning *Grief Diaries Anthology*
Founding partner, International Grief Institute

"If your love of reading lives at the intersection of friendship, faith, tenacity, intergenerational connection, and humanity, this can be an important memoir for you. Don't wait. Add it to your library today."

George H. Schofield, PhD
Named a Top Influencer in Aging
by nextavenue.org, a digital platform by PBS
Author of *How Do I Get There from Here?*

"*The Power of Friendship* is a charming walk down memory lane in the midst of facing current realities. This delightful memoir weaves together past and present, taking the reader on a unique and yet universal journey of two 'forever friends.' The faith foundation that undergirds it all is especially inspiring, as Marilyn shares honestly about her relationship with God, and desire to listen and follow the prompting her prayers reveal. This book is a must-read for any women's group that is looking for a quality story that will inspire reflection and encourage the sharing of one's own friendships and the life experiences that have shaped them."

Rev. Elizabeth Testa, MDiv
Women's Transformation and Leadership
and Equity-Based Hospitality
Reformed Church in America

"Not only is *The Power of Friendship: Lessons Learned from Lifetime Friends* a revealing and intimate book about friendship, it also demonstrates the peace and strength that faith brings to believers. Carol and Marilyn model the meaning of true friendship and the art of aging well."

Mershon Niesner
Certified Life Coach,
Author of *Mom's Gone, Now What?*
and *The Bootmaker's Wife*

"Reflections, perspective, and God's faithfulness are squeezed out of these stories and trips down memory lane. The heart-warming thoughts in this book will be an encouragement to your spirit."

Dan Seaborn
Founder and President of Winning At Home, Inc.

THE POWER OF
friendship

LESSONS LEARNED *from* LIFETIME FRIENDS

MARILYN LUTKE EMERY
with Carol Ford Jennings

Published by HigherLife Development Services Inc.
PO Box 623307
Oviedo, Florida 32762
www.ahigherlife.com

ISBN: 979-8-9859212-5-0 paperback
ISBN: 979-8-9859212-6-7 ebook
Library of Congress Control Number: 1-12904440601

Printed in the United States of America.
10 9 8 7 6 5 4 3 2 1

dedication

*This book is dedicated to our husbands,
Arthur Emery and Charles Jennings.*

They showed unconditional love through giving constant encouragement and showing genuine interest while Carol and I wrote the continuation of our lifelong friendship journey.

contents

foreword

I
n reading the *Power of Friendship*, I was reminded time and time again of God's knack for sending friends into our lives to bless us. The friendship between Marilyn Emery and Carol Jennings tells a story about the power that is togetherness. These two friends have shared the joys of life together and have carried the burdens of life together as well. Simply put, these two sisters in faith embody what Christian friendship ought to look like. The natural depth of their friendship moved me to consider the depth of my own friendships. In a world that is so often self-seeking and individualistic, Marilyn and Carol narrate a friendship that is selfless and beautifully interconnected. To be sure, this book is as refreshing as it is counter-cultural!

I was also moved in this book by the sacrifices these two women made for one another for the purpose of caring for each other at various life turns. The great German theologian Dietrich Bonhoeffer once defined a friend: "A friend is someone who possesses and implements an irrational commitment to the well-being of someone else." Their irrational commitment to each other becomes evident in this book. So much so that their love for each other can only be Christian. With great enthusiasm, I commend this book to others as an inspirational and uplifting read!

— Rev. Dr. Mark Williams,
Senior Minister, Naples United Church of Christ

introduction

Our first book, *The Promised Piece: The Inspirational Journey of Two Lifelong Friends,* is the backstory Carol and I used as we continued our journey forward.

This second book has three parts: The past, the present, and the future.

PART I: The Past – Our Lesson

This section of the book reveals the promise that Carol and I made to each other after she suffered a stroke in 2005. Together we recorded our lifetime journey, recalling our friendship years from young schoolgirls and crafting how we fulfilled the promise made to each other in our early retirement years.

Carol and I initially met for park bench conversations after her stroke. We focused on her rehabilitation from the debilitating stroke which she had experienced and miraculously survived. We also discussed our families, the Draco group of sisters, and our Lee High Class of 1960 reunions. Included are the lessons we learned from the past.

PART II: The Present – Our Gift

Upon initially meeting with Diane, our agent, we felt extremely confident about what she had proposed. In fact, Carol and I were so confident that we made the decision to extend our story by adding facts about our present-day lives.

We decided to continue meeting for park bench conversations in both Florida and Michigan. Carol and I have continued to explore new parks and casually share our life experiences. We feel blessed and excited to continue our valued friendship journey, which we view as a gift from God. Topics discussed are family times, golden retirement, upcoming health issues, senior moments, and our ongoing park bench conversations. Friendship events spent with our special Draco sisters, and the class of 1960 reunions, became our primary focus.

PART III: The Future – Our Motivation

The future is in the form of touching spiritual pieces written by our forever friendship group, to include Pastor Dale Kronemeyer, a former classmate, and Rev. Dr. Mark Williams.

We humbly envision our future with spiritual meditations, which give us personal motivation to prepare ourselves for God's purpose for our lives.

Our purpose is to continue to live our lives in the moment, and to focus on our everlasting future with our Lord and Savior.

We invite our readers to join us on our extended friendship journey as Carol and I further discovered stronger love, faith, hope, purpose, connection, and God's perfect peace during the early 2020s.

the draco girls

BACK ROW: (LEFT TO RIGHT)

Marcia VanTil Stuit – (Tilsie) Best friends with Donna. Sandy's cousin. Surgical registered nurse. First Draco sister to pass away in 2012.

Susan Robson Zuidema – (Sue) Best friends with Sandy in their adulthood. The widow of Ron, who died of COVID in 2020. A mother and a grandmother. (Just prior to the book's publishing, Sue passed away on August 15, 2023).

Judith Geelhoed-Walkotten – (Judy) Has been married over sixty years to Rich. As an only child, she and Rich ended up with a family of 64! Judy's favorite hymn is "Count Your Blessings."

Marilyn Lutke Emery – (Lucky) The author. Marilyn has a positive outlook on life. She writes, loves God, cares about others, and makes things happen. She was widowed but is now married to Art. She is a mother and grandmother. Marilyn's best friend is Carol.

Carol Ford Jennings – (Ford) Book contributor. Carol is enthusiastic and energetic. She has been married for over fifty years to Chuck and is a mother and grandmother. Carol is always ready to go, and excitement awaits!

Barbara Warren Francis – (Barb) was a leader, persistent, and always involved. Mother and grandmother. Barb loves sailing. Draco sisters have fond memories of her parents, including the boat rides on Lake Michigan provided by Mr. Warren.

FRONT ROW: (LEFT TO RIGHT)

Sharon Kiel VandeGevel – (Share) is musical and strong. The wife of Mel and a mother and grandmother. Sharon enjoys laughter and has a very solid Christian foundation.

Jacqueline Ainsworth Seinen – (Jackie) is sweet and giggly. Worked as a nurse. She is a widow, but happily engaged in God, family, and life.

Sandra Van Ark Katsma – (Sandy) Marcia's cousin. Was happy and always wore a smile. She was the second Draco sister to pass away (2023) and is survived by her husband, Bob, her children, and grandchildren.

Donna Baar Tillema – (Baarsie) Best friends with Marcia. Fun, caring, and always sharing. She has a fine family and a God-loving and giving heart.

PART 1

a friendship journey
(the past)

our lessons

CHAPTER ONE

a promise made

An Emergency Trip to New York

Was she still alive? I prayed fervently that Carol would hold on.

My husband, Art, and I packed our car on a sunny July day in 2005 and drove from our summer home in northern Michigan. Our destination was Saint Joseph's Hospital in Syracuse, New York. Although it was a beautiful Sunday afternoon, it was not a planned pleasure trip.

Instead, an extreme medical emergency prompted us to drive to New York.

After spending the night in Ohio, we got up early Monday morning with a goal to arrive at the hospital in the afternoon to be with Carol Jennings, my forever friend since elementary school. The life of one of my longest and dearest friends was hanging on the precipice of life and death. As a newer retiree at the age of sixty-two, Carol had suffered a debilitating stroke which left her partly paralyzed.

After the diagnosis that she had suffered an ischemic stroke, usually caused by a blood clot that blocks or plugs a blood vessel in the brain, the medical staff had given Carol the intravenous (IV) tissue plasminogen activator (tPA), commonly called the "clot buster." Then there was a forty-eight-hour window in the critical care unit where she was closely monitored. Her health could rapidly deteriorate, or God would pull her through the debilitating stroke she had experienced.

While traveling, my mind kept pleading with God to permit Carol to survive the stroke. If I had a lifeline with Carol I would whisper, "Please be strong, Carol. I need to see you, pray with you, and give you hope. Hold on, you can do this, dear friend."

In total desperation, I prayed, "Dear God, please permit Carol to survive this critical forty-eight hour waiting period and heal her according to your will. Give her the strength to fight for her life. May she feel Your tender love as a warm beacon of hope surrounding her. Thank You, Father."

Having prematurely lost my husband to death eleven years prior, and my mother had recently passed away, I was unprepared to face another death situation. No, not Carol! Not my forever friend. My head couldn't go there at this moment in time as we drove the lengthy distance to New York.

It seemed as though the Lord was trying to tell me something, prompting me to listen. I tried to hear Him but was too upset and couldn't comprehend the message. I felt a persistent nudging and the word "promise" kept repeating itself in my mind.

Please, Lord, reveal what the word "promise" means.

The trip seemed endless as we headed toward Syracuse. At last, we arrived and registered into the same New York motel where Chuck, Carol's husband, and two of their adult sons were staying. After unpacking the car, we took a few moments to catch our breath, before driving to the hospital.

Saint Joseph's Hospital

As Art and I walked to the entrance of Saint Joseph's Hospital from the parking lot, relief swept through me. We had safely arrived. However, I was concerned about Carol. Was she still alive? If so, would she be able to recognize us?

Art knew that I was stressed. He said, "Honey, Carol will be glad that one of her longtime friends came to be with her. Don't worry. We will bring her encouragement, and the Lord will bless Carol. He will give you the words to say."

I had been taught both from the Bible and from my parents not to worry, but to give it all to God. I knew in my heart that He would take care of things in His way and in His time.

Since receiving the call about Carol's stroke, everything seemed surreal.

As planned, Chuck met Art and me in the front entranceway of the hospital. He embraced us, told us how the stroke occurred, comforted us, and gave us an update of what was currently happening.

Before escorting Art and me upstairs to Carol's hospital room, he explained that since Carol had survived the first forty-eight hours, she was moved to a shared semi-private room with another stroke victim.

His "Dolly" (Chuck's endearing name for Carol) would be seen by therapists today, evaluated, and rehabilitation would start immediately.

Chuck explained that a blood clot on the left side of Carol's brain caused the stroke, leaving her paralyzed on the entire right side of her body. He added that due to nerve damage, the right side of Carol's face was drooping, her right hand was frozen, and she had severe weakness in her right leg. She also had problems with speaking.

Chuck told us that Carol would recognize us, but we would have to do the talking, embracing, and everything for her. She could use her left hand and seemed aware but was frustrated that she could not move around independently or verbally communicate.

The sooner Carol responded to the physical, occupational, and speech therapy, the better her chances were for successful rehabilitation. He further explained that stroke patients make the most progress the first year after the stroke.

As we took the elevator up to Carol's room, I was grateful that she was still alive. However, I was not prepared to see my forever friend in this condition, lying in a hospital bed with only one side of her face looking slightly the same as when I'd last seen her.

Carol's left side looked normal, but the right side of her face and body only slightly resembled my longtime friend whom I have known and have held dear for so many years.

Appearance didn't matter one bit. Without hesitation, I went to Carol and hugged her. A nurse settled her into a more comfortable sitting position. As I watched, a tear trickled down Carol's left cheek. I tried to concentrate on that side of her face and body and wiped the tear from her chin. It was obvious that her right side was not responding in a like manner. No tear or normal facial expression was detected due to muscle weakness.

Carol gave Art and me a tight hug as she grabbed for our hands with her left hand, obviously glad we had come to visit. She seemed confused that she couldn't speak. It was also difficult for her to drink, swallow, or even eat soft foods.

This was now her "new normal," and I could tell that Carol was not pleased with this condition. Her body language revealed how she felt. She seemed somewhat anxious.

I quietly told Carol that Art and I wanted to be with her, so we immediately drove to New York on Sunday afternoon after Chuck had called us. She squeezed my hand. I was relieved that she seemed to comprehend what I was saying. The feeling of acceptance was mutual because being there for each other is something we both understood.

Two of the Jennings' sons were in the hospital room. David and Scott had flown in from Michigan. Mark, their third son, would soon be flying to Syracuse from Colorado. The sons spoke with us and made a point of including Carol in the conversation. Although she couldn't respond, the inclusion allowed her to feel part of the group.

Later, Art and I ate dinner in the cafeteria with Chuck, David, and Scott. I didn't like leaving Carol alone in the hospital room. However, I knew she needed to rest.

Visiting Carol

The next day I requested some "girl time," because I wanted to speak alone with Carol and present her with some gifts. I had been praying steadfastly to the Lord to keep Carol safe, so I could arrive and speak with her. God was still trying to tell me something, and I kept listening but wasn't sure of the message until I sat alone with Carol. The Holy Spirit gave me the words.

First, I gently washed Carol's face with a warm washcloth. Then, I tenderly massaged moisturizer on her face, neck, and hands, which seemed to relax her. After brushing her hair, she squeezed my hand and started to sob. Carol was upset because she couldn't do these simple tasks for herself.

As I held Carol's hand, I explained that she would soon be able to wash her face, use moisturizer, and brush her hair again. Of course, Chuck would have to assist her until she was able to care for herself.

I presented Carol with a bouquet of flowers from the Draco sisters, our forever friends from Lee High School. After placing the vase on her bedside table, I explained that the sisters were praying for her. They sent their greetings and love. I then showed her the book, *Divine Secrets of the Ya-Ya Sisterhood*. One month before Carol's stroke, the Draco sisters had lunch together and had seen the movie.

Carol seemed happy with the mini-spa treatment and the gifts.

Our friendship meant the world to both of us, and it was such a relief that Carol was still alive. In my heart, I felt certain that God would heal her, and she would work hard to survive this debilitating stroke.

I said, "I've been working on writing my family memoir. God directed me to put that project on hold for now, and to write a story about our lifetime friendship journey. Together, you and I can write a book about our friendship." Since Carol appeared to comprehend what I was saying, I continued. "Carol, I will need your help. It's our prayer that you survive this stroke, which will allow you to assist me by sharing ideas as well as the steps you will take during rehabilitation."

Not only was Carol attuned to what I was saying, I could tell how relaxed and happy she seemed as she grabbed my hand and shook her head in a positive "yes" motion. We both understood that when Ford (Carol) and Lucky (me), used our Lee School nicknames, and when we agreed about something, it was going to happen. The vow we made to each other was sealed with a hug between two forever friends.

A tear slowly trickled from the corner of Carol's left eye. She closed her eyes.

Carol

I lay on the bed with my eyes shut tight. I wanted to spend time in the security of the darkness to digest everything Marilyn had said about the two of us writing a book about our lifetime journey.

Marilyn and I are going to write a book about our friendship and the journey we have taken and are now taking. I can hardly speak, but with faith in God and with the love and help from family and friends, we can do this. Yes! Marilyn and I are going to write our friendship story.

Lesson: God's spirit moves us forward in the face of adversity.

Sharing the Promise

We made our promise, as Carol was propped up in a hospital bed in Saint Joseph's Hospital in Syracuse, New York, on July 18, 2005. I knew years would pass before the fulfillment of that promise would take place. I also understood that the word "promise" would eventually be used in our friendship book. Perhaps for the title of the book or for a chapter title.

We sensed the Lord's presence as we made our vow to write a book together. There was no doubt about it. Carol and I felt the strong bond which would enable us to fulfill our promise of writing about our inspirational friendship journey. Our vow was worth more than silver or gold. It inspired us to fulfill the promise we made to each other.

I helped her get comfortable and continued holding her left hand as she shut her eyes. I solemnly whispered, "Thank you, God, for our friendship. Please lead us as we write the story of our lives together. If it is Your will, give Carol strength as she rehabilitates and courage as she survives this stroke."

Relief swept over me. I realized the burden I had carried regarding what God was trying to reveal to me had manifested itself in our hospital room conversation. The words I spoke to Carol about writing a book were what God had been trying to tell me, but I couldn't grasp the meaning before.

After covering my friend with a blanket, I saw that she was sound asleep, so I went downstairs to join the men in the cafeteria.

I told Chuck I had given Carol a mini-spa treatment, and I would teach him how to do the same. Chuck had no daughters, so this would be a stretch, but I knew that he would do anything for his Dolly.

Then I explained that Carol and I had promised to write our lifelong friendship story together. I told the men that we sealed our vow with a hug, and one tiny tear had rolled down Carol's left cheek.

I said, "It is my intention to start writing the book, and when Carol is ready, we will work in unison on the project. Since God directed me to write our story, He will lead us to finish this project."

Art and Chuck understood. I wasn't sure what David and Scott thought about our vow.

However, I felt confident that a book would be written, and that our promise would, in time, be fulfilled.

Parting for a While

A few days later, Art and I told Carol we were leaving to drive back to Michigan. She seemed to understand that she had weeks of difficult therapy ahead of her before being discharged from Saint Joseph's Hospital.

Chuck was in the process of making flight arrangements for Carol to be transported by a private medical evacuation plane to Mary Free Bed Rehabilitation Hospital in Grand Rapids. Upon her discharge, Carol would face an undetermined amount of rehabilitation in Michigan.

As we said good-bye to Carol, she said her first clear word, "Art!" I could hardly contain the joy I felt that she had spoken. Instead of crying or saying something jubilant, I smiled and told her that I would soon see her in Grand Rapids.

I placed a quick kiss on her forehead, then hurried to the hallway where I cried happy tears for her one word ... and sad tears because I suspected that Carol had many years of difficult rehabilitation ahead of her.

Chuck walked Art and me to the parking garage. He explained that Carol had to undergo therapy, and the specialists would evaluate the situation before allowing her to fly home. Medical staff would be on the plane with Carol and Chuck. The boys planned to fly home to their families and jobs in Michigan on a commercial flight. Mark, their youngest son, would fly to New York and drive his parents' car back to Michigan.

Chuck asked me to phone or email Carol's close friends to update them on what had transpired so far. He promised to keep me informed on what was happening, so I could pass the information on to others. As soon as the plans were in place, he'd let me know the date of Carol's arrival back in Grand Rapids at the rehabilitation center.

Chuck's love for Carol was more than obvious. He made sure he knew what was happening by communicating with the medical staff and therapists.

On our way back home, a heavy weight lifted off Art's and my shoulders. God had brought Carol through the critical forty-eight hours. Soon she would be on her way home and continue her rehabilitation in a city where many people knew and loved her and her family.

Lesson: When you feel called to do something, pray about it, and then do what you feel in your heart.

Significance of the Promise

When I think of the word "promise," I recall the pledge that God made to Noah and his descendants. The Lord promised that He would never again allow a flood to destroy most living beings, and a rainbow was a visible sign of God's faithfulness to His word. Perhaps Carol's and my promise to write a book would represent our rainbow in the future.

God stands by His promises. Humans have good intentions, but often are unable to keep their promises as planned. Would Carol and I be able to write and publish our lifetime story? Would her health allow her to participate in this project? Would I be able to write this story and have it published to make our promise come to fruition? These questions ran through my mind.

The one thing I knew was that God had nudged me to write Carol's and my inspirational story. With His guidance, we would complete our book with the goal of bringing love and hope to all those reading it. But more significantly, the book would represent gratitude to God for healing my lifetime friend.

If our children, grandchildren, and future generations read our story of growing up in the 1950s and 1960s, we would be gratified. Our descendants would surely get a sense of the wonderfully exciting and yet innocent experiences that we, Ford and Lucky, had participated in during our educational years at Lee High School, and how that friendship continued into our senior years of life.

It is our hope that many readers will receive our positive message of love, hope, and the importance of lasting friendship. We are fulfilling a promise made in a hospital room in 2005. A promise between two mature lifelong friends.

The story we are crafting is special to us and to the people we love. These people are part of the rich soil of our youth and are included in the harvest of the past, present, and future years of this ongoing journey.

However, if it was ordained that other readers receive our message of love, hope, and the importance of lasting friendship, perhaps the positive message would be an inspiration for others.

Charting Our Course

Our inspirational story began when Carol and I met in elementary school in the late 1940s and continued through our growing-up years during the 1950s. It included our maturing years of college, marriage, and raising families from the 1960s to the 1990s, including our career years, which finally brought us to our retirement years. We have been privileged to spend time together in Grand Rapids, Michigan, and southwest Florida, as well as traveling with our husbands in our retirement years.

Carol and I had park bench conversations as we crafted our ongoing story. Our Draco sisters and classmates were included as we continued meeting for outings and reunions. Technology has kept us connected throughout the years.

We have felt blessed through the development of this project and appreciate the articles that the Draco sisters and a few male classmates have been asked to contribute. Carol and I are excited about this extended version of our journey, as we face each new day.

K-12 Lee High School building

CHAPTER TWO

the past years

Growing-Up Years

"**M**arilyn, someone is at the door for you!" My mother yelled from the bottom of the stairway. I was upstairs in my bedroom, so I hurried down. There stood Carol Ford at the side door.

She was my classmate in the fifth grade at Lee Elementary School.

"Hi, Marilyn. I just moved to the corner of Delwood and Chicago Drive. We're close neighbors now. Let's start walking to school together, okay?"

"Yippee!" I yelled in my fifth-grade voice as I went outside to join Carol. We continued talking. We had been students together since kindergarten, and both of our families had moved from Berkley to Delwood Avenue, one block from our former homes. My family lived at our new residence for one year, and now the Ford family had also moved to our block.

We rode our bikes up and down the block as I pointed out where Wendy and Tom, our classmates, lived. Also, I pointed out the church parking lot where we played softball and the corner woods where we rode our bikes on the trail.

My home was a two-story house with a huge screened front porch. Just down the street, Carol's ranch-style home sat on the corner.

She took me inside to meet her mother and her grandmother, and then we went on a tour of their home. She showed me the huge double-stall garage.

What truly amazed me was the knotty pine paneled downstairs, which included a large recreation room complete with an office, laundry room, bathroom, and a room full of sleeping bags and pillows for Carol's future overnight slumber parties.

Lee Elementary School

Each school day, Carol and I would walk to and from school together in rain, sleet, and snow. The five blocks didn't seem very long because other neighborhood friends often joined us on our jaunt to Lee Elementary School.

The Godfrey-Lee School experience was special because people in the community were friendly. Many of our parents had attended Lee School, and it seemed as if everybody knew each other.

Ours was a bedroom community which covered just over a mile. Children could safely walk to the library, drugstores, athletic stadium, and local churches in the neighborhood.

There was a feeling of safety and friendship everywhere you went in the Godfrey-Lee K-12 School District, not only at the school, but in the stores, restaurants, businesses, and churches. The community radiated a caring attitude, and therefore, we grew up in an extremely protected atmosphere.

Carol and I would walk to a small store just a few blocks away for a loaf of bread or a gallon of milk for our mothers. There was always a penny, nickel, or dime left over to buy a gumball from the machine, a candy bar, or for ice cream at the local Dairy Bar a few doors away.

I don't remember exactly when it happened, but as we walked to school, Carol called me "Lucky" because my proper last name was Lutke, and I called her "Ford," her last name. It stuck with us for years, and other classmates started calling us Ford and Lucky as well.

Middle and High School Years

Ford and Lucky walked to K-12 elementary, middle school, and finally to high school together. We were friends, neighbors, and classmates until our high school graduation in June of 1960.

Ford and Lucky's 6th grade class

We also walked to the football and baseball fields on Godfrey Avenue, to the new gymnasium for basketball games, and each Saturday we walked to the small gym for scheduled group roller skating. First, skating was in the afternoon, but as we began eighth grade, we skated on Saturday evenings with the high school students.

When we decided to visit downtown Grand Rapids, we walked to the bus stop to catch the bus, or we would walk to the Soda Bar on Chicago Drive for a Cherry Coke and fries. It was fun to go with a group and listen to the fabulous 50s tunes on the jukebox at the Soda Bar after evening activities.

The speakers blared out all the popular songs, and the noise level kept getting more intense as the teens competed with the music. We would sing and talk with the volume becoming louder and louder.

It was a safe place to be with a group of LHS teenagers who were seeking fun and companionship as our relationships continued to grow stronger.

Our favorite music included Elvis Presley, Fats Domino, Pat Boone, Bill Haley, Patsy Kline, Connie Francis, the Everly Brothers, the Supremes, and other artists. Students enjoyed ballads, pop, some country western music, but mostly rock 'n' roll music in the 1950s.

Going Downtown

When we became eighth graders, Ford and I had permission from our parents to take the bus downtown. In our minds, that made us pretty mature as we wandered around Monroe Street through all the department stores. The main stores were Wurzburg's, Steketee's (Stek's), Herpolsheimer's (Herp's), and even to Jacobson's (Jake's).

Carol and Marilyn "goofing off"

After shopping, our next stop would be at Carol's father's shop on Fulton Street called Smalley Daniel's Bike and Cycle Shop. We continued walking back to the bus stop located near two dime stores, Kresge's and Woolworth's.

Ford and I would order a Cherry Coke as we sat at the lunch counter, and sometimes we would buy a small bag of potato chips. When heading home, our last purchase was some warm cashews from a machine to snack on to quench our hunger pangs before dinner.

If time permitted, Carol and I would put a quarter in the small photo machine located near the front door of the dime store. After closing the curtain, we would pose and make ridiculous faces, then wait for the finished product to spurt out. We would laugh at our goof-off smiles and actions. We couldn't wait to show the small pictures to our friends at school the next day.

On our half-hour bus ride home, Ford and I discussed our shopping experience and shared opinions about our favorite department stores.

"My favorite store is Herp's because it's located close to my dad's bike shop," Ford said. "After I shop, I like to buy a chocolate ice cream cone in the store basement. Sometimes Mom and I come downtown to eat dinner with Dad when he works until 9:00 p.m. Mom and I go to a movie, shop, or get our hair cut before we meet Dad."

I said that the best time to go downtown was at Christmastime when all the lights are strung, and the store windows are decorated. Carol listened as I told her that my sisters and I used to go to Wurzburg's to see Santa, and when we were younger, we would ride Santa's Rocket Express, the elevated train in Herp's basement.

With memories surfacing, I added that my mom took me and my three sisters downtown where we loved seeing the lights, hearing the Christmas carols, and slurping on chocolate ice cream cones.

We both agreed that the chocolate whipped ice cream cones at Herp's was the best reason for visiting downtown Grand Rapids. We also would enjoy an occasional movie, eat a snack, and go to the Santa Claus Parade, which was held before Christmas on Monroe Avenue. If it snowed, everyone felt very excited. Several bands marched in the parade. I marched with the LHS band, but just being a spectator sitting on the sidelines also presented wonderful memories from the past.

The hottest children's ride in town! Santa's Rocket Express
Image Courtesy of the Grand Rapids Public Museum

Reflections

The vision of rich soil, constant nourishment, much pruning, and the development of fine products remained in my thoughts. Even as young girls, Carol and I appreciated the fact that we grew up in a caring community where people took pride in their family, schools, churches, neighborhoods, homes, and businesses in the Lee High School area.

There was love for our country which was personified by a huge American flag on a pole outside the front of the Lee School building. The Pledge of Allegiance was repeated each day in individual classrooms in the elementary schools. Students put their right hands across their hearts, as they felt a pride in God, our country, and our American flag.

During our public-school years, we often whispered a silent prayer before eating. We also attended a Bible club on our lunch hour or after school without any negative connotations.

Once we were in middle school, we girls would take the bus downtown as a group. It was our custom to shop at the department stores, shoe shops, or dime stores. Sometimes we went swimming at the local YWCA or saw a favorite movie, and we would buy a treat prior to returning home.

Before being able to drive in high school, the Draco girls took the bus downtown for various purposes such as to work on a research project at the Grand Rapids Public Library or attend a display at the local museum. We also attended a variety of lectures, concerts, or special events at the Grand Rapids Civic Auditorium. We stayed together and usually stopped to get something to eat at Holly's or Howard Johnson's restaurants before returning home.

When going downtown, the memory of attending the Civic Auditorium for an early Easter Sunrise Service instantly entered my mind. The girls from our church group were dressed to the nines with our Easter outfits which included hats and shoes to match.

After a pastor preached a touching Easter message about Jesus' resurrection from the grave, the entire auditorium burst into a huge choir singing "Christ Arose." Then the pastor continued preaching about Jesus' resurrection from the grave and that He lives forevermore. The entire auditorium would echo, "Christ has risen! He has risen indeed!"

When we left this service, we went to our own churches for another Easter service. Although that was several years ago, specific touching memories still linger, and have a special place in my heart.

As Ford and I walked back to Delwood Avenue from the bus stop, we would say, "Bye, friend. See you in the morning," as we walked to our separate homes.

Draco Sisters

When young girls meet new friends during their early elementary to high school years, seldom do these friendships remain over a lifetime. Never would Carol or I have guessed at that time that our group of friends would become our lifetime sisters. The roots that were planted when we were youngsters were deeply embedded, and as the roots became stronger, so did our wonderful friendships.

The Draco girls knew each other from kindergarten at either Godfrey or Lee Elementary Schools, and after connecting in the eighth grade, we continued our close friendship in high school.

We attended Draco Horizon Club meetings and often walked to and from most extra-curricular activities as a group. Although we lived in a safe community, our parents preferred that we stayed together as a group, especially for evening functions. Roller skating, ice skating, sock hops, and slumber parties on Friday nights after football and basketball games were some of our favorite activities.

Lesson: Friendships formed at a young age can become even more solid over the years.

Beach Time

Swimming and sun tanning on the beaches in Michigan were part of the Draco girls' most fun times. When we camped or rented a cottage on Lake Michigan, we would rent bicycles or walk the Grand Haven and Holland fishing piers.

When hungry, we walked into Grand Haven for Pronto Pups or root beer floats at the local food stands. We attended church on Sunday morning, and if it rained during the week, we saw a movie on Washington Street in downtown Grand Haven.

Holland Beach was where the Draco girls tented. One year, Sue invited four of the girls to stay in her family house trailer on the oval in Holland. The other girls stayed in a large tent a short distance away.

Mr. Warren, Barb's father, met the Draco girls in Holland and took us waterskiing on Lake Macatawa. We then traveled through the channel into the "Big Lake" (our name for Lake Michigan) for a rather bumpy boat ride.

Often Lake Michigan was too cold and wavy to ski on, so we would climb the sand dunes. Although trudging up the giant dunes was a chore, we would sprightly run back down and dive into the chilly white-capped lake.

Forever Friendship Piece

Draco Horizon Club: Barbara (Warren) Francis

The Godfrey and Lee elementary schools had Bluebird groups for second graders who "flew up" and became Campfire Girls. The Campfire Girls became a Horizon Club when we converged at Lee School in the eighth grade.

In the spirit of togetherness, the girls united. Since the combined group was too large, we split into two groups, each with a mixture of Godfrey and Lee girls. We dubbed our group "Draco," the name of a constellation.

On occasional weekend evenings we Draco girls and our dates would go as a group to the Wilder farm for hayrides. Following the bumpy ride (there wouldn't be much straw left on the wagon), we would enjoy barbecue beef sandwiches and hot chocolate, and we would talk and dance.

The Draco Dog Constellation

The high school walls were papered with posters announcing Draco projects and social events. Secretly, we

called ourselves the Draco Drips and sometimes still do. The Drips were a very busy lot.

Draco sponsored the first after-game sock hop held at the school and put together yearbook signing parties. Members did community service work, and these skills helped us in our future endeavors.

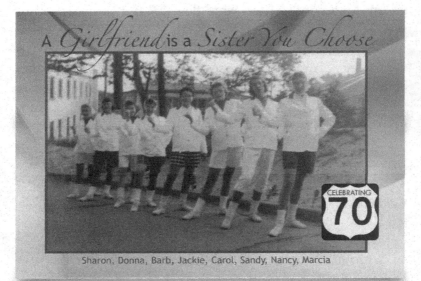

A *Girlfriend* is a *Sister You Choose*

CELEBRATING 70

Sharon, Donna, Barb, Jackie, Carol, Sandy, Nancy, Marcia

Draco girls at Grand Haven Beach

Summer Fun

The Draco girls rented the Eagle's Nest, a cottage on the oval in Grand Haven, just steps from the beach on Lake Michigan. We spent a summer week there before our junior year, and another prior to our senior year of high school. Besides having fun, we learned excellent skills for working together. These group dynamics helped us as we continued in life.

In our senior year of high school, the varsity basketball team made it to the state finals. Draco girls and basketball players painted my car gold and blue, the LHS school colors.

The students who worked on the project thought it was a work of art and emblematic of our winning spirit.

The basketball players signed their names on the car alongside painted Rebel flags. We were known as the Lee High Rebels.

After the games, we would join a victory parade of cars through downtown Grand Rapids.

The entire community was caught up in the excitement of the winning basketball season, and the spirit continued throughout the year.

Barb Francis and I had many fun times at LHS as classmates and especially with the Draco group. Her parents were community-minded and were loved by the Draco girls. (Mrs. Warren was our leader, and Mr. Warren took the girls boating and waterskiing.) Barb and I were neighbors for quite a few years during our adult years. She has recently experienced several health issues with surgeries and follow-up therapy at Mary Free Bed Hospital. Our prayers are for Barb's health, so that she is able to enjoy several more years.

CHAPTER THREE

a weekend
at the cottage

Before Carol's Stroke

My husband, Art, and I had driven north to our cottage on Lake Leelanau, in northern Michigan. We anticipated a weekend of relaxation on the waterfront and meeting some relatives on Sunday for a brunch after church.

Friday afternoon was spent walking along the marina and the beach in Traverse City, and then a quiet enjoyable dinner ended with watching the boats sailing on the Traverse Bay.

Saturday morning was spent at the cottage relaxing as we viewed the lake from our front deck where we ate and read. A walk followed in the afternoon, and we went to Leland's Historic Fishtown Village where we dined. Following dinner, Art and I walked along the channel where the fishing and sightseeing boats are docked. The old fishing buildings were visible, and the smell of fish permeated the air, as we window-shopped at the small boutiques. We then walked the Leland marina docks to get a glimpse of the pleasure boats and beautiful harbor with views of Lake Michigan.

We could never have anticipated that this peaceful weekend would suddenly be disrupted. The ringing of the phone awakened me early Sunday morning and ended Art's and my quiet weekend. I'll never forget Carol's husband's pronouncement.

"Marilyn, this is Chuck, I am calling from Syracuse, New York. When Carol and I were preparing to leave to drive back home to Michigan, she had a stroke." His voice was low. I was startled, as he continued.

"After our appointments in Boston, Massachusetts, for physical examinations at the Lahey Clinic, Carol and I drove to New York and spent the night at a motel in Syracuse. The next morning, I went outside to pack the car to leave. When I returned, I found Carol. She had suffered a stroke in the motel room.

"I called the front desk and told the hotel staff to call an ambulance to take Carol to the nearest and best hospital in the area, which was Saint Joseph's Hospital."

My tired mind could not comprehend the message Chuck relayed. I felt weak as he continued talking. Although my ears were hearing the words, my heart could not accept the message. In fact, I may have been in shock as I listened. Finally, I asked in almost a whisper, "Chuck, is Carol alive?"

There was quite a long pause ... then Chuck said softly, "Yes, Carol is alive. She had an ischemic stroke and is paralyzed on the right side of her body. She can barely speak."

Tears streamed down my cheeks. I wanted to be there with Carol because her parents are deceased, and she is an only child. I *needed* to be there for her.

My words and my heart were miles apart, yet I was relieved that Carol was alive. My cheeks were getting warm. I couldn't accept all this sad news so early on this beautiful summer morning.

"Thank you for calling, Chuck." My voice quivered. "I will let our close friends know what you told me, and prayers will be rising as soon as the sisters hear what has happened. We love Carol and you. We will be with both of you in spirit and through our prayers."

After we hung up, I took a deep breath, washed my face, and relayed the facts I had just learned to Art through tears. After sketching a phone tree, I began making phone calls. I called my closest friends first, asking them to call others, so all the Draco women and other close friends would be notified.

Church

Art and I quickly dressed and drove to Leland to the Methodist Church where we met my father, sister, Joanie, and her husband, David. They had saved seats for Art and me as we planned to worship and then go back to Joanie and David's summer home for a brunch after the church service.

I chose to be in the Lord's house that Sunday morning. I needed to pray and to be with my family. They had known Carol since her childhood, and they had seen her less than a year ago at Art's and my wedding and reception.

Upon reaching the pew, I choked up as I told my family about Carol's condition and asked for prayers for her and the Jennings family.

Dad and Joanie grabbed my hands. They were as distressed as I was. They knew Carol well because she had been a fixture at our home growing up. They had as much difficulty taking in the news as I had an hour before.

After church, we drove to Joanie and Dave's beach home in North Port. Before brunch, Dad prayed the most beautiful words I have ever heard flow from his lips. He asked for God's strong, loving, and tender arms to be wrapped around Carol so she would feel the warmth and see the light of His glorious countenance around her.

Dad could pray so eloquently and in such a meaningful way. Joanie and I held hands because we are close and, therefore, she had known Carol well and understood how much Carol has always meant to me.

Lesson: Do not worry. Put your trust in God.

Months and Years Later

After surviving the first forty-eight hours, Carol had been transferred to a semi-private room in Saint Joseph's Hospital where rehabilitation began immediately. I recall that Carol took a particular liking to her young speech therapist, Marie. That relationship prompted Carol to listen closely to instructions and to work her hardest at speaking clearly.

"Marilyn, my little angel … was Marie, my … speech therapist who … was very kind and … I knew immediately … that her intent … was to help … me to speak again. She came to meet … me in my hospital room … and wrote her name … on the white board. Then … she explained that we … would be working … together to get … my speech back."

Carol liked Marie instantly. She pushed herself to work extra hard for Marie. The first time they had met, there was a certain bond that prompted Carol to listen and try to please her.

Marie had done an initial evaluation on Carol and noted that she had met Carol in the intensive care unit on July 16, 2005. She also recalled that Chuck had been right by Carol's side observing and asking questions.

We asked Marie to give an overview of how she assessed Carol in her journey to obtain spoken language.

Marie said, "It was clear that Carol's ability to express herself was significantly impaired. Her spontaneous speech was limited with some nonsensical words. Carol was able to complete simple automatic speech tasks (i.e., counting) but phonemic errors (sound substitutions) were present. This frustrated Carol because she knew what she wanted to say, but her words weren't clearly expressed.

"She also had trouble swallowing foods and liquids safely, which initially required altered food and liquid consistencies. Carol's emotions ranged between frustration, fatigue, and sadness. These, however, never got in the way of her fight to communicate to become independent again."

Marie added, "Carol's family, Chuck and their sons, are a wonderful support system at this difficult time, and they will also be there for her in her long journey ahead."

Carol progressed to producing short sentences with some phonemic (sound) errors by the time she was ready for discharge. She was being medically evacuated to acute rehabilitation back in her home state of Michigan. Her ability to eat and drink safely had improved, and she was able to eat regular solid foods and liquids. These accomplishments set the stage for her continued recovery.

Upon discharge nine days after the stroke, Chuck had promised to keep Marie updated on Carol's progress, and he diligently kept that promise.

One day, five years after the stroke, Carol phoned Marie. It was a special moment for both women. Carol thanked Marie for helping her and told her that she was her "angel." Carol also explained the progression which had taken place over this span of time.

Hearing Carol speak clearly caused tears of joy and excitement for Marie. "It's a glorious day!"

Marie, who is now married and the mother of two young sons (and still a speech and language pathologist), explained that Carol and she have continued to keep in touch.

Periodically, they even see one another. Their special bond has continued to this day.

Marie said, "No one would have guessed that devastating, life-altering day would have blossomed into a wonderful bond between Carol and me."

When Carol speaks of Marie, she smiles. Indeed, Marie was and still is her special angel.

CHAPTER FOUR

informative years

Family Facts

While we attended Lee School, Carol would stop by my house, and we would walk the five blocks to school together. Sometimes Sue, Nancy, and Sandy joined us as we took our daily ventures on Engle Street to the Lee Elementary, Middle, and High School which were all located in the K-12 building.

"Where were you born?" I asked Carol one day as we walked to school shortly after she moved to Delwood Avenue.

Carol said her parents moved to Grand Rapids from Big Rapids, Michigan, where they had grown up, so she was born in Grand Rapids. She mentioned her father's bicycle, cycle, and repair shop in downtown Grand Rapids.

We found it interesting that both of us were born in Grand Rapids.

I explained that my mother grew up in East Grand Rapids, and my father moved to Grand Rapids from the Cadillac area when he was young. We both had spent our past years in southwest Grand Rapids, and we travel north to Big Rapids and Cadillac to visit relatives.

When Carol asked me about my father's job, I told her that Dad was a builder and he had worked as a carpenter until he went to Ypsilanti, Michigan. He worked at the Willow Run World War II bomber plant to help with the war effort in the early 1940s.

Dad was drafted into the United States Army as a tanker in 1943. He took a ship over to Europe and was gone for two years. He was part of General Patton's Tank Corps and was active in the Battle of the Bulge.

At that time my older sister, Joanie, and I were called "war babies." When our father left to serve his country overseas, my sister was almost three years old, and I was eighteen months old. We learned more about World War II as we grew up. Our father would share his war experiences with us. Our entire family praised God when Dad, our uncles, and other military friends returned safely home and settled into civilian life.

Carol's father did not serve in the military because he had back problems, so he stayed home to run his business. Her Grandfather Ford was a bank president in Big Rapids. She enjoyed visiting her five cousins, who lived on Chippewa Lake near their grandfather's home.

I knew where Big Rapids was located because we drove through the small town on our way to visit relatives in Cadillac.

The Lutke family had a boat named Lucky Seven, and Dad took us for boat rides. We also fished at various inland lakes. Dad loved to fish, hunt, and boat in Michigan.

As I think back on those years, I recall that Carol often wished she had sisters and brothers. She mentioned that there were times she felt lonely being an only child, so she enjoyed all the bedlam at the Lutke home. As I mentioned, Joanie was my older sister, and my two younger sisters were Jan and Marcia, whom I often babysat. My baby brother, Tom, was born when I was a sophomore in high school. It

Marilyn welcoming her dad home from WWII

was extremely busy at the Lutke household with much noise and confusion when compared to the Ford home.

A packed car with seven family members going to church on Sunday mornings and evenings, celebrating with relatives on birthdays and holidays, heading to the Lake Michigan beaches, or camping was a way of life for the Lutke family. It was heaven for me to go to Carol's house and listen to music, play card games, and just hang out without the many distractions taking place at my home.

Family Travel

As children, trips were mainly taken to see relatives in Michigan. I remember trips to other surrounding areas—Indiana, Illinois, Ohio, Louisiana, and Canada—with family. As teens and young adults, New York, Florida, Kentucky, and California were destinations points, as well as Mexico. My first European trip was as an adult taking ocean and river cruises.

Television Sets

In the 1950s, a black and white television set was found in almost every living room across America. Many of the sets had an antenna on top, and the picture was not always clear. The outdoor roof antennas helped to clear the snowy television screen, and we were so happy to watch a spectrum of shows on the three channels offered at that time.

Men usually favored the news and sports shows, while women often enjoyed the *Arthur Godfrey Show* and afternoon soap operas. Younger kids favored cartoon shows and *The Howdy Doody Show*. Carol and I loved *Lassie, Roy Rogers, I Love Lucy,* and *Mickey Mouse Club*. As teens we watched the Dick Clark *American Bandstand* show after school. On the weekends, we looked forward to watching *The Ed Sullivan Show* and *Your Hit Parade*.

When guest singers appeared on the shows, teens were excited to see the stars, especially Elvis Presley, who was a favorite in the 1950s and 1960s. Teenagers thought Elvis was cool when he swayed his hips to the famous rock 'n' roll music. Other rock stars would also appear, causing great excitement.

Journaling

While growing up, I wished I had more free time to quietly write and reflect. In middle school, I had a five-year diary with a little key. I would hide it so my siblings couldn't share this little-bit-of-something that was just mine.

Years later, Carol mentioned that she too started journaling in a five-year diary when younger, and then we both transferred over to notebooks. Carol had journaled over the years until she had the stroke.

I wrote my reflections in steno notebooks, which I dated and put into a box in a remote corner of the downstairs storage room. When I married, moved, became a mother, during my career, my first husband's death, became a grandmother, remarried, and retired, I continued journaling. Even decades later, I still daily record my experiences. Many times, I've reread precious memorable moments, feelings, or have gone back to these journals to verify specific details of dates and trips.

It's a legacy to have these personal records which perhaps no one else will ever read. For now, they belong to me alone. Which reminds me that these notebooks—hidden in a box—may contain yet another story which may someday appear. Perhaps in a family memoir just waiting to be written in the future.

Lesson: Stay close with friends who share the same values as you and who also share the love of God.

Activities

Carol and I were active young students at Lee High School (LHS) and we belonged to various clubs. Carol was in the choir, and I was in band. We remained active with our Draco Horizon Club. Other school clubs included Girls Athletic Association, Future Teachers of America, PEP Club, Y-Teens, and being on both the Ariel and Echo staffs, which were the school newspaper and yearbook organizations. We held officer positions, served on committees, and were ready to volunteer when needed.

We cared about our grades, studies, and liked staying active in our separate church groups as well. Our lives were well-rounded. The conversations we had on daily excursions included the boys we liked and dated. Also included were our teachers, the classes we were taking, future college plans, places we dreamt about traveling to in the future, and the people we would like to meet in our lifetime.

Styles of the 1950s

Fashion was important, but the choices were not as vast as they are today for students.

Although we didn't wear uniforms, our high school clothing consisted of skirts, blouses, and sweaters. Slacks were not allowed at LHS during the school day. Girls could only wear their jeans, sweatshirts, and casual wear after school.

Most commonly, bobby sox were worn with penny loafers or saddle shoes and sometimes knee-high socks with pleated skirts. Flat shoes and heels were worn for dressy days or on important occasions.

For formal dances, the girls wore floor length net formals or mid-calf taffeta cocktail dresses.

Our accessories included long white gloves, pearl necklaces and earrings, dressy heels, fancy hairdos, and make-up.

1959 (Sue Robson, Fran Bailey, Marilyn Lutke, Sharon Kiel, and Sandy Van Ark)

Prior to a formal prom, the girl was presented by her date with either a wrist corsage or a floral corsage that was pinned on her formal. The guys received a fresh rose or carnation boutonniere worn on the lapel of their white sport coat. Their attire was complete with black bow ties, trousers, and black dress shoes.

The Senior Trip

Homecoming dances and proms were the highlight of our junior and senior years, and the senior trip to Washington, D.C., will never be forgotten. Our class took the Chesapeake & Ohio Railway from Grand Rapids to our national capital in Washington, D.C.

Part of the itinerary included touring multiple historical museums, presidential homes, the United States Capitol Building, the Lincoln Memorial, and the Arlington National Cemetery. The class enjoyed being together viewing various places, and we saw the award-winning *Ben Hur* movie. The class and our chaperones ate at fancy restaurants and stayed in a historic hotel.

Meeting Gerald R. Ford

The highlight of the trip was when the class had an arranged meeting with Representative Gerald R. Ford, from Michigan.

He led our class on a tour through the Capitol Building, explained about the chambers, and had his picture taken with the Lee High School class of 1960. It was an educational day. Since many of our parents were schooled in Grand Rapids, they remembered that Jerry was an outstanding athlete. He and his wife, Betty, were raised locally. Therefore, the LHS

LHS seniors meeting Gerald R. Ford on class trip to Washington, D.C.

students felt a close relationship with Gerald Ford and his family.

Later, Ford became the speaker of the house, vice president, and president of the United States. Jerry, as locals knew him, had grown up in Grand Rapids where he played football at South High School and at the University of Michigan in Ann Arbor.

The Gerald R. Ford Presidential Museum is located in downtown Grand Rapids, which overlooks the Grand River. President Ford and his wife, Betty, are buried on the grounds of the museum in the city where they both grew up and which they loved.

Looking back at the senior trip, our classmates thoroughly enjoyed a week of travel together in our nation's capital. We will forever have these memories.

Graduation

In June of 1960, eighty-two proud graduates received their diplomas at Lee High School.

After the graduation ceremony, we attended our individual family parties and stopped to see our favorite classmates at their homes. By the end of the day, we were excited and tired at the same time.

We understood that our lives would change as we stepped out into a new and different world.

Post-High School Years

Many students from our graduating class went to college and later became degreed.

However, some classmates chose to get jobs, others went into the Armed Forces, while some married and soon started families.

The Draco group of girls went in various directions as some chose to attend college and earned degrees in nursing, education, and business. Others found jobs in business, and a few married shortly after graduation.

As Carol and I were packing for a Holland Beach week with the girls after graduation, I said, "Hey, Ford, I decided to go to Grand Rapids Junior College for two years before attending a state university. What are your plans?"

Carol decided to do the same, attend Grand Rapids Junior College. But first she wanted to go to the beach with the girls, and then seriously contemplate upcoming fall college classes at another time.

A few months later, both of us attended GRJC. We rode to the downtown campus with our friends Barb and Sharon.

Lesson: Good friendships can last forever even though you don't see each other every day.

Forever Friendship Piece

Friendship: Sue (Robson) Zuidema

This is what I remember about the Draco girls' lives together as friends. Marilyn and I go back a little bit further than most since we were neighbors on Berkley Avenue until her family moved a block away to Delwood Avenue.

I don't recall spending much time in the early years—kindergarten through seventh grade—with the girls who would become the "Draco Drips." Most of these friendships started when the Godfrey kids came to Lee School for their junior high and high school years.

The girls in the Draco Horizon Club seemed to blend as sisters from the start. We did pretty much everything together. During the school year, we celebrated our birthdays by going to the house of the birthday girl for a special luncheon or to Carol's house for a Friday night slumber party.

46

Mr. Warren, Barb's father, took us waterskiing in the summer, and we also had many beach parties on the beaches of Lake Michigan.

Then there were the candy stripers, nurse aides. We received volunteer training and then worked at Saint Mary's Hospital in Grand Rapids. Out of that experience, the medical field gained two dedicated nurses, Marcia and Jackie, from our group.

Now we are in our golden retirement years, and I think we realize the reassurance we have with these special sisters. They know and care what happens to us and to our families. A lot of people can't fathom our unique friendship. Acquaintances ask, "You have been friends for how long?"

Sue was my first friend. We walked to school together because we lived on the same block in our early elementary school years. After I moved, we were in the Draco group together. Sue married Ron, also a graduate of LHS, and they have a fine family living in the Grand Rapids suburbs. Ron passed away from COVID in December 2020.

(Just prior to the book's publishing, Sue passed away on August 15, 2023).

CHAPTER FIVE

mary free bed rehabilitation hospital

Carol's Rehabilitation

After spending nine days in Saint Joseph Hospital, Carol flew in a medical evacuation plane from Syracuse, New York, to Mary Free Bed Rehabilitation Hospital in Grand Rapids, Michigan. Chuck flew with Carol, along with medical personnel, on the trip home.

It was a relief when Carol arrived in familiar surroundings at the rehabilitation center where she received therapy after the stroke. She had a private room and used a wheelchair to navigate around the hospital.

However, she was determined to work diligently to get out of the wheelchair so she could walk again and become as independent as possible. She wanted to become the Carol she used to be.

Her constant prayer was, "God, please help me to walk, talk, and to be able to live a useful life in the future. I know that You are the center of all existence, and I pray for the strength to be normal and healthy again."

Chuck had requested that no friends come to visit until Carol got acclimated to the new hospital setting and schedule. I let the girls know. They respected the guidelines, of course, but were excited that Carol was back in her hometown.

After I received Carol's schedule, I let the LHS girls know so they could visit and not interfere with her rehabilitation, meals, or rest periods. The girls looked forward to being with Carol and giving her positive feedback on her journey back to wholeness.

Once the visitations began, her family and friends were there for her. She spent nineteen days in that facility. Carol claimed to have worked harder at the rehabilitation center than she had ever worked before.

Therapy

Physical, occupational, and speech therapists met with Carol daily when her rehabilitation program began.

One day when Carol spoke to me, I noticed that she was starting to sound more like her old self. Determination was in her voice as she said, "It is … hard work, Marilyn … I push myself … because I … want to … go home. I need … to get out … of this wheelchair … into my own house … and make my … own decisions. I know Chuck will … help me. All … I long for … is to be … normal again … to be the old Carol."

Carol steadily improved. There was one last activity which she had to perform before being discharged from the rehabilitation center. That was to take her therapist and Chuck to lunch, order from the menu, and pay for the food herself.

A few weeks later, she invited me to lunch, and we went to the hospital cafeteria. The only thing that frightened me was the fact that Carol often choked when she ate. I knew that medical personnel would be available, but thank God, we didn't need any assistance that day.

Carol and I laughed and talked and had a wonderful time. There was much improvement in her talking, walking, and in her flexibility at that point. However, once she was discharged from rehab, there would still be several sessions of outpatient therapy for months to come.

"I'm ... so excited ... to go home ... to Spring Lake ... and to sleep ... in my ... own bed ... and live ... more of a ... normal life ... again," Carol said.

Sharon, one of our longtime LHS friends, and I visited Carol one day at the rehabilitation center, and we walked alongside her wheelchair to the therapy room. We observed as our dear friend diligently worked to do everything the therapist told her to do.

Sobs of frustration could be heard as she strived to perform all the therapeutic exercises correctly. Sharon and I wished we could do the therapy for Carol. It was at this moment that we realized the tough, long, and frustrating road our forever friend still had to travel.

Home to Spring Lake

After three weeks of stroke therapy, Carol was allowed to move to their Spring Lake condominium on the Grand River. Chuck continued driving her to outpatient services at Mary Free Bed three times per week, and Carol worked super hard during that time.

Chuck helped his Dolly walk and shower. He assisted her when she dressed, cut her food, and would give aid in any way possible to make Carol's life more pleasant. He was a loving and patient caregiver and often asked Carol how he could assist her. He even wrote in her journal as she eventually found words to dictate to Chuck. He penned them for her until she learned to print with her left hand.

On one of Art's and my visits to Spring Lake, the guys went to do some errands. While they were gone, Carol shared with me that she wanted to do more things for herself. It was her desire to become more independent. She also said that she wanted to have more time to herself.

That was a "WOW" moment. The look on Carol's face told me that she was ready to take on the world alone and would only need some assistance from others for specific things.

When Carol shared her feelings with Chuck, he listened to her request and gave her more space. He began to go shopping, attend luncheon engagements, and made appointments. He felt better about leaving Carol for longer periods of time.

Sometimes the four of us would go out to lunch or dinner. We would wait until Carol had finished eating as much food as she could before allowing the staff to clear the table. Someone had to cut the meat on her plate. She was primarily using her left hand but certainly making progress.

When I was alone with Carol in a restaurant, I would wait for her to ask me to cut her meat or to assist her in any way. I once forged ahead to be helpful, and she called me "Mother." Another time, I was giving her directions to input information on a computer with her left hand, and Carol called me "teach" or "teacher." This told me that I was overcompensating for her and that she could do many things herself.

Rehabilitation was a learning experience for both Carol and me. When I watched her struggle, I sometimes found it difficult to step back and let Carol do things her own way, in her own time. But I understood the process, and she had made excellent progress every time I saw her.

One day while visiting, Carol asked if I would bring the recording of Art's and my wedding reception for her to hear. She wanted to compare her old voice, when she gave the matron of honor speech a few years earlier, to her current voice. I told her I would look for the recording, which I found weeks later. When I heard the difference in Carol's voice, I didn't know if she should hear the change between her old and new voice.

When I brought the recording to Carol's home, at her insistence, we sat alone and listened to her speech. Tears welled up in Carol's eyes. I felt horrible. Her voice was lower and less vibrant now. She was obviously surprised at how much the quality had changed.

It was part of Carol's therapy to try to improve the tone of her present voice quality.

Years Later (2010)

About five years after Carol's stroke, she was able to relay more facts about her rehabilitation at Mary Free Bed.

"My lasting memories are of the doctors and therapists who worked with me. And especially the visitors, and all the love that was shown toward me. It was remarkable how dedicated the staff was and how amazing family and friends were in cheering me on as they showed so much love and care. The staff, my family, and my friends were truly amazing by helping me gain back my strength. I was fortunate that so many well-trained and qualified specialists and therapists worked with me after I became a stroke victim."

Carol was especially thankful to Dr. Chris, a physiatrist who helped her to verbally admit that she had suffered a stroke. This was the beginning step to mentally heal from this debilitating stroke.

Kristi, Carol's occupational therapist for outpatient therapy, also was a significant person in helping her to become more agile, and to be patient in her journey back to living a normal life again.

Kristi said she felt fortunate to have met Carol and her doting husband, Chuck, and that the couple made a special mark in her heart.

Whenever Carol had yearly outpatient appointments with Dr. Chris, Chuck and she would find Kristi and show her the progress Carol had made. It was a very positive thing for Kristi to see just how much Carol had advanced.

Kristi said, "They would give me a big hug, and then we would review Carol's therapeutic progress since I last saw her. She would show me new movements her arm could make, or how she could use her left hand better for a simple task like picking up a finger food. The three of us shared a bond of therapy and Carol's recovery.

"From the beginning of Carol's therapy when she presented with left hemiplegia, it was difficult or almost impossible for her brain to tell her right hand or leg to move in ways we each take for granted. My focus was her right arm which had no movement or activity in the extremity.

"Our treatment began at her shoulder. We used various instruments to elicit movement in the right shoulder. Her elbow, wrist, and fingers would flex without Carol's volitional control. A resting hand splint was made for Carol's right forearm, wrist, and hand, and she also trialed a stretch splint. She would wear the orthosis each night to bed.

"Gradually, she gained strength and active movement of the shoulder, then her elbow, and finally the forearm and wrist."

Kristi said, "Each time they came for a treatment visit, Chuck was on the sidelines, cheering Carol on and pushing for more—more movement and more function. Chuck often challenged Carol or me as a therapist to assure gains."

Carol and Chuck became special friends to Kristi, even after she no longer needed to help Carol work on her arm. "I can now glow in Carol's progress and watch her gains as she moves into a new and wonderful chance at living and enjoying her life."

After hearing these statements, Carol was proud of her continued progress. She felt a great sense of accomplishment for what she had achieved during her rehabilitation.

Outpatient Care

Carol and Chuck lived in the lakeshore area which was their home in Michigan for approximately thirty years. They originally lived in the greater Grand Rapids area, but in their empty-nest stage, they moved to Grand Haven and lived in a condominium overlooking the channel leading to Lake Michigan. Their next move was to a home on Spring Lake. In their retirement, they moved to a condominium located in the Village of Spring Lake on the Grand River.

Carol was happy to be in her own home after leaving Mary Free Bed Hospital. She was familiar with everything about their condominium. Living with Chuck again in their own place gave her a feeling of comfort, and now she was ready to start being more independent as she started making great strides.

Chuck drove Carol to Mary Free Bed for outpatient therapy three times per week, as well as to speech therapy in Grand Haven and eye and dental appointments. They went out to eat quite often with family and friends.

Not only could Carol go out socially, but she passed a driver's training class and test and could drive again. A necker's knob (used with one hand) attached to the steering wheel enabled Carol to make turns as she still didn't have complete use of her right hand.

Heading South

Carol requested to have therapy appointments made in Naples where they wintered. She had attended outpatient therapy sessions for three years.

She said, "I was very excited about returning to Florida in the fall. The warm weather was a blessing as I grew stronger. I felt healthier in the warmth of Florida."

She had already tried light therapy, Botox injections, and a series of acupuncture sessions, but these sessions were not helpful. Thankfully, the neuromuscular physical therapy sessions helped her hips, and walking became easier for her. The therapist truthfully told her that her right hand would not improve. Carol had to digest this bad news.

She did not give up, though. Instead, she started doing everything she could with her left hand, while her right hand became her helper hand. She became more capable with her left hand as it grew stronger. It was at this point, however, that she decided to try therapy one final time on her right hand, to improve movement.

Carol decided to go to a special restraint therapy clinic in Alabama to see if she could regain some use of her hand. The therapists restricted her left hand, which forced her to use her right hand, and they worked with her for hours at a time. She did the therapy for two weeks. Although it helped a bit, in the final analysis, she came to terms with the fact that her right hand would never heal completely and that her new normal was to use her left hand and arm for almost everything.

Thankfulness

When Carol verbalized her feelings and told me details about her stroke, I was grateful. I valued and appreciated each bit of information she shared with me. I realized that by sorting ideas, it forced Carol to think and to speak, thus comprehending the details about her recovery.

My prayer had been that God would protect Carol through rehabilitation and would give her strength to survive. I also gave Him thanks for putting the correct medical doctors, specialists, therapists, and nurses in the right places at the right times. This was paramount on Carol's journey back to health and happiness.

2006 – Interview and Picture

Mary Free Bed is the nation's most comprehensive rehabilitation provider and one of the largest nonprofit, independent rehabilitation hospital systems in the country. Therefore, it was such an honor that of the hundreds of patients who had been cared for at this facility, they chose to spotlight Carol for their annual awareness campaign.

She was interviewed by Mary Free Bed and asked, "If there is anything in the world that you would like to do, what would it be?"

Without delay, she said, "I would like to be able to dance with Chuck again."

Carol's gift was granted. She and Chuck were selected for a Mary Free Bed advertising campaign, where they were showcased dancing on billboards. Their picture appeared in *The Grand Rapids Press* and on television commercials to prove that anything is possible after surviving a stroke.

Mary Free Bed Promotional Campaign

Mary Free Bed "Dance" Promotion

"I left the hospital in a wheelchair. Today, I'm dancing with my husband again." During an out-of-town trip, Carol Jennings suffered a debilitating stroke. She and her husband, Chuck, knew the reputation of Mary Free Bed Rehabilitation Hospital, and she was flown back to Grand Rapids for her rehabilitation. Carol spent three weeks as an inpatient in the stroke program, followed by intensive weekly outpatient therapy. She worked tirelessly with the occupational and physical therapist to regain the use of her right leg and arm. What was her motivation? Carol was determined to walk, then to get back on the dance floor with Chuck.[1]

Paying It Forward

Carol's family and friends are so proud of her, and the fact that she keeps trying to improve her skills. She was relentless in striving to be as normal as possible. Her positive attitude and happy disposition were helpful throughout her therapy and in her daily life.

The thing that I especially noticed was Carol's urge to help other stroke victims. She and I call it our "pay-back time." We discussed how happy it makes us feel to help others and to see others survive something we endured ourselves.

Volunteer Work

Years after Carol's stroke, she did some volunteer work at Mary Free Bed Hospital and gave information to patients. They realized that she too had been a patient at the facility years before and could see how well she functioned. It gave them hope.

As time went by, Carol felt comfortable visiting stroke patients in their homes. She told them of her past experiences, with the goal of giving them encouragement.

---

1   https://www.maryfreebed.com/

Carol said, "I gain much satisfaction by continuing to stay involved in life and by finding new avenues to give back to others and hopefully to enrich lives."

The same way Carol spends time with stroke patients, I spend time with widows who need a patient and listening ear and a kind heart, as they are trying to survive the death of a dear husband.

I have done various types of volunteering: in the theater, well-baby clinics, an adoption organization, a child study group, a hospital guild, and for various church organizations.

However, never have I felt such a mission as giving back to new widows who are grieving.

After being a young widow myself, I found it was part of my inner-being to reach out to grieving widows in a personal way. By going out for brunch or lunch, listening, and having an understanding heart, I found much gratification in helping others the way I had been helped in the past.

When it comes down to making a difference in someone's life, you must look for a way to give back. That is what life is all about.

Lesson: Speak words of kindness; it will come back to you in endearing ways.

CHAPTER SIX

the LHS class of 1960 reunions

Memorable First Reunion

The class of 1960 continued staying close. We have enjoyed class reunions every five years since 1965. The first reunion was held at a camp facility on Lake Michigan overlooking Holland Beach. It was a very casual buffet, and the classmates and their mates/dates had a fun evening.

Reunions are something our class eagerly anticipated.

Only a few reunions are highlighted in our story, however. Our class had met at various places including lodges, halls, country clubs, hotels, and restaurants for the past sixty years.

In fact, when the class of sixty turned sixty years old, we held a 60/60 dinner as a mini-reunion. We thought that was a perfect reason to celebrate in between our normal five-year reunions.

Pastor Dale Kronemeyer, our classmate from Arizona, keeps the class together by planning mini-reunion luncheons and/or dinners in between the five-year class reunions when he and his wife visit Grand Rapids.

Somehow the strong roots which were deeply embedded in the 1940s have held tightly as they have been nourished over the years. The rich soil has produced a strong yield, and consequently, the closeness of our class of 1960 remains years later.

Twenty-fifth Class Reunion

As Carol and I reminisced about our class reunions, the twenty-fifth came to the forefront of our minds. It was a special reunion held at the Amway Grand Plaza Hotel in Grand Rapids in 1985.

Several of our classmates were in attendance. Some of them had traveled from different states to attend this event. It was mostly a time to meet and greet each other, and we presented each classmate with a booklet featuring everyone's personal updates. We mailed an advance questionnaire asking for each classmate's address, phone number, and details about their family, job, travels, and additional information that they cared to include.

After an excellent dinner, we enjoyed a short program. The visiting went on late into the evening. It felt good to be together again and to see how members of our class had matured over the years.

We had not lost any classmates at that time. It made us aware that life is very precious and to enjoy each moment.

Destination Reunion

In 2005, our class had a destination reunion at the Homestead Resort in Glen Lake, in northern Michigan, to celebrate our forty-fifth class reunion. Many couples spent the weekend at the resort, and we had a wonderful time kayaking, hiking, golfing, and of course socializing and eating many meals together.

Carol had suffered the stroke just two months prior to this reunion, so she was unable to join us. I brought Carol some souvenirs, such as a program and pictures from the reunion, and explained the photos to her. This was the first class reunion Carol had ever missed. She hopes to never miss another one in her lifetime, because as an only child, the class is Carol's family.

Also, just before the forty-fifth reunion, one of our classmates, Bob Hoffman, had passed away, and the class was heartbroken. We were beginning to lose members and missed them at these gatherings. Although death is a reality, it is hurtful as our class numbers become smaller.

Fiftieth Class Reunion

In 2010 the fiftieth class reunion was held over a September weekend in Grand Rapids. The Friday evening casual dinner was held at a pole barn. Before we gathered there, the class met at Lee High School for a tour of the school. Many things had changed over fifty years. We were pleased to see a huge newer cafeteria and computer labs.

After the tour, classmates headed southwest to a pole barn in Byron Center which belonged to Donna's family, one of our classmates. We enjoyed a casual barbecue.

Dinner was followed by entertainment. I presented a lip-sync presentation of the song, "I've Got You," by Patsy Kline,

LHS Fiftieth Class Reunion

complete with an old Ricky Nelson record album and a 1960 class ring as props. Lynda Reynolds, Marty's wife, and her sister sang and played guitars. It was a fun evening.

We met again the next evening, Saturday, for a formal dinner at the Crowne Plaza Hotel in Cascade. Two of our past teachers/coaches were in attendance, Bob Wright and Dwayne (Tiger) Teusink, and they spoke after dinner. Our Draco sister, Marcia (Van Till) Stuit, gave an overview of our class accomplishments over the years. A group picture was taken outside of the hotel to commemorate this very special milestone reunion.

We were thrilled that Marcia had given the presentation at our fiftieth class reunion because little did we know that two years later she would pass away as a result of stage four cancer. We will remember Marcia and the joy she gave to so many people.

Fifty-fifth Class Reunion

Five years later in 2015, the class held its fifty-fifth reunion at the Railside Country Club in Byron Center, a suburb of Grand Rapids. The club is located on a beautiful golf course. After registration and a cocktail hour, everyone was seated.

Before dinner, Marty Reynolds, the chairman of the reunion committee, welcomed everyone and handed the microphone to Rev. Dale Kronemeyer, the pastor representative of our class.

Dale updated us about our classmates that had passed away. Approximately one quarter of our class were now deceased. Dale read the name of each departed classmate as a memorial.

He then gave the invocation, and the class enjoyed a nice meal. After dinner, I gave an overview of Lee School, from its beginning, called Green School in the 1800s, to the Godfrey-Lee Public School System, which has remained the same for many years. Lee School is located on Lee Street Southwest, and the students have been known as the Lee High Rebels since 1923.

In 2020, Lee High School changed its mascot name from the Rebels to the Legends. This will take some time getting used to, especially for the alumni who were known as the Lee High Rebels for over ninety years.

News Item

I had asked Doug Greenwold, a class member and former athlete in our group, if he would announce the induction of class member, Marty Reynolds, into the Baseball Hall of Fame.

Then it was time for the class of 1960 to play a trivia game whereby clues were given until each classmate present at the reunion was identified. In turn, the class member would stand and introduce their mate and share something about their family, where they presently live, retirement, travels, and other interesting information.

We are like one big family, looking forward to each reunion as a wonderful occasion to be together. The reunion was successful, and we looked forward to our next one, which would be our big sixtieth class reunion in 2020.

Committee Meeting

Marty, the chairperson of the class reunions, called a meeting of the committee in June 2019, a year in advance of our sixtieth reunion. Upon meeting at Marty's condo, he was the only male classmate in attendance. Bob had a heart problem and had been hospitalized, and Dale, our communications chairman, lives in Arizona.

The committee decided on a date in September 2020 for our 60/60 event. The class of 1960 would be celebrating our sixtieth reunion in the fall which seemed to be the best month for our class to unite.

We came to a consensus that we liked the location and setting of Railside Golf and Country Club where we held the last reunion. Not only was the club centrally located and close to hotels/motels, but the food was also good, and the clubhouse was comfortable with a lovely view.

We secured the date with a reservation, and a save-the-date email was sent to our classmates.

Lesson: Enjoy every possible moment with friends; one never knows how many remaining years we will have together on earth.

Forever Friendship Piece

Special School Friends – Sandy (Van Ark) Katsma

I like the idea of always having good friends available for group activities. The Draco girls had fun-filled times at the Eagle's Nest cottage in the summers during high school.

Getting together twice a year for luncheons with this group of longtime sister friends is something I look forward to. Also, our LHS reunions every five years are special times for the entire class, and the dinners between reunions are a bonus.

Due to health issues, Sandy could not submit a written piece. She shared her thoughts in a conversation with Sue, her closest friend in the group.

Sandy lived one block west of Carol and me growing up and she often walked to the high school and various places with us. Carol and Sandy were in the LHS choir together. Gloria, Sandy's older sister, often chaperoned the Draco girls on group events. Sandy married Bob, a classmate, who was the president of our senior class in high school. They have two children and several grandchildren. Sandy lived in a memory unit for seven years and passed away on February 14, 2023. We shall miss her sweet smile and kind heart.

CHAPTER SEVEN

initial park bench conversations

Return to Florida

Carol and Chuck returned by car to Naples, Florida, in October after she had attended many outpatient therapy sessions at Mary Free Bed Rehabilitation Hospital. The staff had scheduled therapy sessions in Florida for Carol so she could continue her rehab over the winter and spring months.

Often Carol would drive to Art's and my condo on Marco Island from her condo on the Isles of Capri, so we could review the book manuscript. We would sit on my condominium lanai, which overlooked the Gulf of Mexico. It was a pleasant way to read and reflect.

I began working on our story after Carol's stroke and when Carol's speech started to improve. She would give me input about her therapy sessions, the women's groups she had memberships in, her church Bible class, and various events Chuck and she were attending in Florida.

These visits helped Carol's comprehension, by thinking and speaking, and it gave me information which I would input from the notes I had taken. Sometimes I would give Carol an assignment, suggesting that she should think about certain subjects such as family, faith, prayer, purpose, and thankfulness as future topics of discussion.

We were two retired friends comfortably seated on a park bench overlooking a small, picturesque pond. The sun usually was brightly shining, birds were wading on shore, and there were wildflowers growing at the edge of the pond. Occasionally, we saw people walking their dogs or riding bikes on the path around the park. It was relatively quiet except for two longtime friends who conversed, laughed, and reminisced about the past years.

Chats

Carol and I always have plenty to talk about on park benches in both Florida and Michigan.

In addition to being happy, busy, Christian women, we feel an attitude of gratitude for being alive and chatting as we sit on various park benches sharing our lives.

Initially, the peaceful park settings seemed to be a place where Carol was the most comfortable and where we both could relax. I would pose questions in an interview style. It didn't seem like work. It was an opportunity for Carol and me to be together, and to enjoy these special friendship moments.

To get our work concluded, we would concentrate for a while, and then Carol would need a break because of her aphasia. This is a neurological condition which causes difficulty with speech, understanding speech, reading, and writing as the result of brain damage following her stroke.

Ice Cream Time

I usually could detect when Carol needed to take a break, and away we would go to Sweet Annie's or Beebe's for ice cream on Marco Island. In fact, now Carol reminds me when we schedule our park bench conversation to leave time for getting ice cream afterwards.

As we eat our treats, our conversation usually concludes on a bench outside of an ice cream parlor. Our park bench conversations end with laughter and enjoyment, and sometimes a tear is shed as we share our stories of old and the memories we hold dear.

The component that has always been present in our ongoing relationship is that we are interested in each other's lives, and we want the best for each other. Therefore, our park bench conversations have always brought us together to spend precious friendship moments. It's the very reason we've remained friends for so long.

Lesson: Friendship is for sharing and caring.

Blackness

"You have often spoken of the blackness following the stroke, Carol. What is the significance of the darkness?"

Carol said, "I remember having this horrible headache before the stroke, and total blackness followed. It was so peaceful that I wanted to continue in that dark state forever. The ambulance ride to the hospital was a complete blur, but Chuck's voice was familiar. I knew he was by my side in the intensive care unit. His words didn't completely register, but I remember being peaceful and feeling comfort in the first room. I didn't want to be moved to another room."

Rebirth

"I would like to address the topic of rebirth," Carol said. "It's like I lived one life and then I had a rebirth after the stroke. I had to relearn everything I once knew how to do. I look at life so differently now. God was in my life before, but now God is in charge of my life. He brought me through the stroke.

"Family, friends, church, and life represent a new meaning for me. Perhaps sitting quietly during the healing process prompted some refocusing on my part, and I found out what truly brings happiness and wholeness. God is the center of everything. He has provided so wonderfully for me following the stroke."

A Movie

"Marilyn, do you remember when we went to the theater in Naples, Florida? We saw a movie about a stroke victim. The man never recovered. This wasn't even a year after my stroke, and the movie was extremely sad. You were sniffling and dabbing at your eyes, and I was feeling extra grateful to be alive and as active as I am.

"After the movie, we discussed the severity of strokes, and I felt favored to be alive to share my experiences with you. Sometimes struggles make you feel more grateful for everything in life."

Missed Class Reunion

"Missing the Glen Arbor, Michigan, destination class reunion was one of the saddest moments of my life," Carol said. "Not being able to attend the event made me appreciate my LHS classmates even more. It was the only reunion I had ever missed, and I want to thank you for bringing me mementos and pictures from the event. I was there in spirit but could not be there in person. I was miserable because I could not complete my duties as the treasurer of the class reunion planning committee."

Full Circle

"Carol, when you speak of coming full circle, what do you mean?"

"Sometimes I feel my life has come full circle because it's so full now," Carol said. "Because I'm an only child, my sisters have always been the LHS girls. My parents are gone, and I have only a few cousins who are scattered across the country.

"However, the Jennings family always brought me full circle. Chuck, the three boys, their wives, and our eight grandchildren, complete our family. Now I have our family, all our friends, two places to live, and marvelous travel opportunities. Therefore, my life has come full circle.

"I owe so much gratitude to God. I thank him every morning when I wake up. The big one—a second stroke—hasn't happened yet, and I'm still alive and vital."

New Normal

"I would like to discuss my new normal state," Carol said. "After years of therapy, my right hand still wouldn't fully work. When my right foot was dragging, I did intensive therapy in Grand Rapids with a neuromuscular physical therapist. The therapist aligned my hips and helped me with my right leg but let me know that my right hand was as good as it would get. I needed to hear and comprehend the blunt information.

"Thank you for the referral to Dr. Scott. He helped you with your injury after your accident and then helped me with my walking. Dr. Scott helped both of us in time of need. He is a saint—and a good-looking saint at that!"

Marilyn's Accident

"Carol, the accident you mentioned gives me instant cause to be grateful. It could have been far worse."

Unfortunately for me, a truck driver put his delivery truck into reverse and backed into me as Art and I were walking on Marco Island. Because I had migraine headaches, inflammation, and muscle spasms in my neck, shoulders, and upper back, several rounds of physical therapy and additional injections were prescribed at a pain clinic. After weekly physical therapy treatments with Dr. Scott and daily home therapy, the pain eventually left my body.

I take great comfort in being pain-free again. God was most certainly present, and my body was resilient. I was completely healed four years after the accident, and I'm grateful.

Carol's Inking

"Carol, what is the significance of your ankle tattoo?"

She looked at her ankle and smiled. "For many years I had been thinking about getting a tattoo, so I talked to people, got recommendations, and thoroughly checked the information

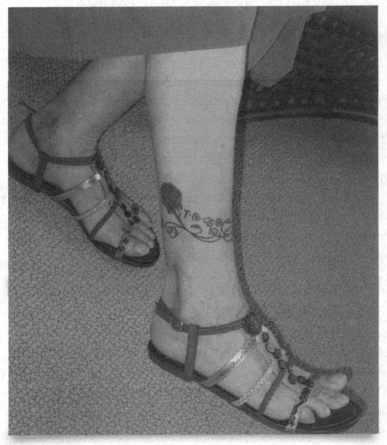

Carol's first and last tattoo, signifying her stroke date

I had gathered. I expected to get a small ankle tattoo showing the date when I had the stroke.

"Finally, I made an appointment with a tattoo artist to discuss the art symbol I desired. I chose a red rose with a fancy black design going completely around my upper ankle. The black design contains the date of the stroke, '7.16.05' and 'CJC' in English block letters for Carol/Jennings/Chuck. Chuck, my soulmate and life partner, accepted the final decision, and the tattoo artist eventually did the inking.

"I like the tattoo, but it's a tad larger than I had imagined it would be. The inking is a reminder that I'm a survivor."

Depression

Carol experienced moments of anxiety before her doctor made a change in her medications.

She explained her sadness.

"After Marcia passed away in 2012, I felt sad. Instead of 'The Ten,' we now have nine LHS girls in our group. I don't want to be the last sister still alive. I feel sorry for the one remaining member who will be alone after all those years of close sisterhood. If a second stroke happens, I don't know that I would care to survive.

"When I come back to Michigan, I think about the years of rehabilitation and about all the people who were dear to me and those who have passed away. Marilyn, it makes me sad remembering our parents, the baby I buried years ago, your first husband, Wayne, our friend Marcia, and other classmates who have gone before us.

"Sometimes the weather is cold and gray in Michigan. I should be used to it, but after a few months, I'm ready to pack and head south to our sunny Florida paradise.

"I wish Mark's family didn't live so far away from us. As you know, his family moved back to Colorado a few years ago. Chuck and I would drive to see him and his family when they lived in Florida, and they could more easily visit us too."

Other signs of anxiety were evident. I would listen to Carol and try to help during her episodes of depression by being there, talking, and suggesting ways to keep busy.

I called Carol in June 2013 after she and Chuck arrived home to Michigan for the summer. "Hey girlfriend, let's meet for lunch at Rose's and then go to Collins Park. We can sit on a park bench overlooking Reeds Lake to chat, walk, shop, and have some fun in Gaslight Village. How does that sound?"

Carol agreed, and after lunch she said, "Sitting in the park is a reminder of when Chuck, the boys, and I lived in this area years ago. I remember meetings and sports activities we attended while living in East Grand Rapids. Being here brings back many memories from younger years with our family and friends."

We decided to go to Jersey Junction for ice cream.

Carol said, "I would like to sit outside and talk just like we did years ago when our kids were growing up. That would bring back old, fun memories, which would be good."

Carol used that as an excuse to have a treat.

We drove to get ice cream and sat outside on a patio bench. Carol seemed delighted to reminisce. As she smiled, a load seemed to lift from her soul.

When Carol's new medication took over, she felt much better. Life in Michigan became enjoyable again, especially in midsummer into the early fall months.

Chuck and I talked about Carol's more positive attitude and concluded that she prefers the warm tropical weather in Florida, which improves her health and her outlook.

The Rhythm of Life

"Carol, what do you mean when you refer to the rhythm of life?"

Her eyes brightened. "High and low experiences are both part of the rhythm of life. When good things happen and life is rosy, that's great! But when negative things happen, we must persevere and never give up on life. That's why I call or visit people who have had strokes. I can help stroke victims by listening to them, by trying to make their lives more positive, and perhaps by sharing my experiences with them."

After giving Carol's words some thought, I realized there is a pattern or a rhythm to many aspects of life. There is a rhythm to every movement, every sentence, every song, every prayer, and every relationship. Of course, not everything in life can be explained or understood.

However, we can gain much satisfaction by going with the flow and realizing that the Lord is always with us even through the twists and turns of life. Being thankful and aware of His blessings helps us to receive and better appreciate the gifts the Lord has given us.

Keeping Positive

"I want to commend you for being such a giving, upbeat, and positive person, Carol. I love those qualities about you."

She smiled and contentment seemed to fill her as she sat on the park bench enjoying the surroundings.

I said, "You not only handle the negatives handed to you, but your fun personality and positive nature shine through. You don't protest or feel cheated that your golden years have been more difficult with the lasting problems caused by the stroke."

Carol explained that although she had experienced difficult moments and had dealt with depression and anxiety, she refused to give up on life. She stands steadfast and dialogues with her medical specialists and with other stroke survivors. Carol enjoys reading books, watching movies, and spending time with friends. One of her favorite activities is attending her women's group meetings in sunny Florida.

CHAPTER EIGHT

through thick and thin

Caretaking

Carol and I often talk about caretaking and the importance that role played in her life following her stroke. "When I think back to the many people who assisted me after my stroke, I am so thankful for each one, and for the time and patience they had with me."

I agreed with Carol that Chuck had a major responsibility serving as caretaker after her stroke, and how organized he was in meeting her needs. She added that she will be eternally grateful for the love and time Chuck gave to her as she survived the stroke.

Thinking back, I recall a friend of mine, Marie, who took care of her aging mother who had suffered two strokes. After her mother passed away, Marie then took care of her husband for years until his death. The first thing on her mind was the care of her mother and husband. There were times she had to turn down social activities because of her responsibilities. She always put her loved ones first.

Marcia, my youngest sister, was a caregiver for her husband, who suffered from a degenerative disease. After caring for him for five years, she had home hospice care, and then made the difficult decision to put him into a skilled care home where he passed away in 2022.

Besides thinking of Chuck, Marie, and Marcia, I think of my husband, Art, who had the sole responsibility of raising his two elementary-aged daughters alone after his first wife passed away.

He was a busy executive who had work and travel obligations. However, his priority was to make sure that his daughters were properly cared for.

Caretaking is a huge undertaking, and God's special blessings to caretakers all over the world who put others before themselves.

Ten-Year Physical Exam

Carol and Chuck had yearly physical exams at the Mayo Clinic in Rochester, Minnesota, after they returned to Michigan in the summer. It had been ten years since Carol had her stroke. Chuck sent me an account by email:

> God's special blessings to caretakers all over the world who put others before themselves.

Carol came through all her exams and appointments with two areas that must be watched regarding her stroke issues. The good news is that nothing much has changed, and she still has enough of an opening in her right carotid artery to supply blood to the brain, but there are several loopy coils in the artery. In other words, in normal arteries there is a straight line, but Carol's has loops. They must be watched, because the blood must travel around a lot of corners as it moves toward the brain. She'll need another extensive exam in eighteen months, and the department head wants to be notified upon admittance to a hospital if there are signs of another stroke.

The other issue is her heart. The valves don't open and close exactly as they should. This results in a little backflow when all the blood should travel forward. The two chambers have to work harder. Otherwise, Carol's heart is good, and all her cholesterol numbers are great.

Mayo Clinic in Carol's Words

Carol called me when she and Chuck returned from the Mayo Clinic. She was elated to be home.

"I'm so relieved that the exam is over. I will continue to exercise in Michigan and do swim aerobics in Florida. The Mayo vascular specialist and department head highly recommended that I should keep in shape so my organs will work correctly.

"Chuck and I will spend the summer in Michigan and will drive to Florida in early October. After staying in Florida for a few weeks, we plan to fly to Colorado to see our son, Mark, and his family at the end of October. The newest addition to our family is due in early September, and Chuck and I want to be there soon after the birth."

New Granddaughter

"Marilyn, I am excited about the birth of Emery, our new granddaughter! Emery Elizabeth was born near my September birthday—ten years after my stroke. She is our eighth grandchild, and her name is spelled the same as your last name. We can't wait to see Mark's family at the end of October when we fly to Colorado."

Leadership Role

Carol explained her involvement in groups in Florida.

"Marilyn, I accepted a new role in my P.E.O., Philanthropic Educational Organization, on Marco Island. I am the new president for 2016–18. When I contemplated accepting the position, both Chuck and you told me that I was qualified and would do a great job. After much thought, I accepted the position. I'll use the gavel with my left hand. I can do this!"

When people see how Carol is ten years after her stroke, they are astonished by the vast improvements that have taken place over the years. Many forget that Carol had a stroke. Instead, they see her positive attitude and her motivation to do an excellent job. With a sparkle in her eyes and a giggle, she carries on to the best of her ability. Carol attended the 150th year celebration in 2019 with two other P.E.O. officers and now serves as the backup chaplain for the 2023–2024 season.

Marco Island

Carol and I decided to continue meeting at the Leigh Plummer Park location on Marco Island. I would proceed by taking notes and inquire about Carol's stroke, gathering further information in a casual way. It was a comfortable setting for having our conversations on this small oasis in the winter months.

On this day, we located our favorite bench under a canopy of trees, and I read from the manuscript. Carol and I discussed ideas that I was considering in regard to finishing the manuscript about our past experiences. Our first story would soon conclude, and I wanted her input.

Carol replied, "Friend, we have covered most aspects regarding the promise we made to each other in 2005. It has been quite a journey from five-year-old children in kindergarten to senior citizens."

We've been known as Carol and Marilyn and many nicknames—Ford and Lucky, C.J. and M.E., Carlita and Marlena, and more recently, Thelm and Lou (our adventurous names from *Thelma and Louise*). We like the tag, "forever friends." We giggled as we remembered all the names we had given each other over the years.

We packed the manuscript into a folder and drove to Carol's condo.

"See you later, alligator," I said as we hugged, and she got out of the car.

"After-while, crocodile," Carol said as she closed the door and waved good-bye.

Stroke Seminar

"Marilyn, let's attend this conference together before Art and you leave for Michigan."

Carol and I attended a women's health forum in Naples on a Saturday morning in April. She picked me up and we headed for the church where the event was being held. Arriving, we checked the booths, had a cup of coffee, and listened to speakers before attendees broke into small groups.

Then, the group met in a large room where we heard Dr. Jill Taylor, the keynote speaker, make her presentation. Carol and I had read her book years earlier and we wanted to personally hear about her recovery from a debilitating stroke. The author brought us through her journey and lectured about the brain and how it works and about the relearning process.

After the seminar, we drove back to my condo parking lot and rehashed the day's events in the car. We both agreed that it had been an excellent morning, a good learning experience, and mostly a time for two friends to be together to learn more about a stroke victim's journey of survival.

Carol felt it was a worthwhile morning. She learned some facts, plus gained names of people who could present at future club meetings. It was such a blessing that Carol was still alive and that we could reflect on her survival and hopefully share information to help other stroke victims.

As I left the car, Carol and I did a high five and said we would see each other in six weeks when Carol and Chuck returned to Michigan. They would fly to Colorado for the wedding of their granddaughter, and then return to Michigan in June.

We planned to get together for a photo shoot with my daughter, Tara. She would take some current photos of Carol and me sitting on a park bench. The plan was to choose a cover photo for the book we planned to write.

Photo Time

In June, when Carol arrived back in Michigan, she came to my home, and because the weather looked threatening, I grabbed two large hats to wear for our park bench photo at Tassel Park in Cascade.

Yes, we needed the hats, but according to Tara, my photographer daughter, the weather conditions were perfect for a beautiful photo opportunity.

Tara positioned Carol and me on the park bench in a beautiful setting with the Thornapple River in the background. We posed and smiled despite the raindrops that were coming down.

Collins Park

Carol said, "Marilyn, let's have lunch at Reeds Lake for a park bench conversation and view the photos."

A few weeks after the photo shoot, Carol and I met at Collins Park situated on Reeds Lake in East Grand Rapids. This was a perfect setting in the summer and fall months in Michigan.

Rose's Restaurant, where we often ate lunch, adjoined the park. After lunch we continued talking on a park bench overlooking the lake. Jersey Junction was a block away, and of course we ventured over there for an ice cream treat on our way home.

Tassel Park picture on park bench

The Grand River bridges

CHAPTER NINE

grand rapids, michigan

Description of Our City and State

Ford and I spent most of our lives in western Michigan. I will offer merely a snapshot of where we live and what our city and state were like back in our youth, and what our city is like to date.

When Carol and I were growing up, Grand Rapids was known as the Furniture Capital of America. Furniture was manufactured in the city, and there were many factories, showrooms, and furniture stores in the area. The city is still a hub for manufacturing office furniture, but many other companies and industries are prospering as well.

Since the mid-1990s Grand Rapids has been noticed and ranks as one of the up-and-coming cities in the USA.

Grand Rapids is the second largest city in Michigan. The city is named for the Grand River, which originates in Jackson, Michigan, and flows through Grand Rapids into Lake Michigan on the western shoreline. The city is often referred to as River City.

Several bridges cross the Grand River in the downtown area. These bridges are lit up at night, presenting a picturesque view of the city.

The view from downtown now includes the S-curve on the expressway which connects freeways and roads throughout the city. Grand Rapids is home to hotels, restaurants, schools, colleges, universities, the Medical Mile, sports complexes, cultural buildings, parks, golf courses, ski and walking trails/hills, John Ball Park Zoo, Blandford Nature Center, towering office buildings, and of course, the Grand River.

Favorite spots we visit along the river are the fish ladder, the river walk, and various parks and bridges. Since Carol's and my childhood, Grand Rapids has developed beautifully around the river with urban areas and suburban neighborhoods and developments.

Grand Rapids was a great city in which to be reared, and it is still known as an excellent place to raise a family. The city has a clean environment, the food is delicious, with outdoor markets, and there are many churches, synagogues, temples, parishes, and a cathedral as places to worship, as well as abundant educational opportunities. There are cultural and recreational offerings, along with various music venues, Broadway, and local theaters, art galleries, and festivals. Much is happening in the city where the Calder Plaza houses the Alexander Calder Stabile called the "La Grand Vitesse," French for "the great swiftness," or also translated as "grand rapids," a sculpture which symbolizes the city of Grand Rapids.

Above all, Grand Rapids offers a camaraderie that is difficult to explain. No wonder Ford and I went to college, had our weddings, and raised our families locally. Most of our children, including many of our grandchildren, continue to live in western Michigan.

Speaking of being proud of your city, Carol and I, along with our relatives, classmates, and other friends, have watched Grand Rapids develop into a vibrant, growing, and successful city in which to live. We feel privileged to have been planted, rooted, and nurtured here, and to see some of our children, our grandchildren, and future generations bloom in the same birthplace where we feel blessed to have been born and raised. The soil in our River City indeed represents a full bouquet of opportunities, respect, and love, from one generation to the next.

Michiganders often put up a right hand to depict the shape of the state's Lower Peninsula, an almost perfect mitten, which often surprises visitors, who smile at this gesture. Most of us point to the palm to indicate where a city is located or where Lake Michigan and other Great Lakes are positioned. There aren't many states that can be duplicated with one hand.

When the left hand is cupped over the right hand, it indicates that Michigan has two peninsulas—the Upper Peninsula (called the U.P.) and the Lower Peninsula (the downstate mitten) where Carol, many of our family members, several LHS friends, and I still live.

The Mackinac Bridge connects the two peninsulas and is the largest suspension bridge between anchorages in the Western Hemisphere. The bridge is often called the Mighty Mac or the Big Mac, and thousands of people walk the span on Labor Day. Some find the five-mile bridge a challenge whether walking, driving, or just looking below at the boats and the activity on Lake Superior and Lake Michigan.

People refer to Michigan as the Great Lakes State, the Water Wonderland State, the state with the most lighthouses, or the motor vehicle manufacturing state. "Pure Michigan," the latest nickname, explains this beautiful state perfectly.

Trips

Carol and I spent much of our childhood visiting relatives in places north of Grand Rapids.

The Fords had relatives on both sides of their family in the Big Rapids area, and they spent many weekends and holidays visiting there in the summer and during the holidays.

The Lutke family often spent time in the Cadillac area with relatives, and we camped at Lakes Cadillac and Mitchell. We also stayed in cottages in northern Michigan and camped at various beaches and parks throughout the state.

Northern Michigan

Traverse City also was a favorite place to camp, especially at Interlochen State Park where the Interlochen Music and Arts Camp for students is located. The Lutke family attended concerts and theater productions there. Many wonderful memories were made.

Mackinac Island is a popular place to visit, especially in the summer and fall months. Since there are no cars allowed on the island, one must take a ferry over from Mackinaw City which is south of the bridge. Another ferry can be taken from Saint Ignace which is north of the bridge, in the Upper Peninsula of Michigan.

The Ford family had also visited the island, so both Carol and I had the experience as children, and now our children and grandchildren have had the same opportunity.

It is fun to ferry over to the island and either walk, rent a bike, or ride in a horse-drawn carriage around the island. That, along with the quaintness of the buildings, plus the homemade fudge, is what makes the experience extra unique.

We recalled the prestigious Grand Hotel, where the movie *Somewhere in Time* was filmed, as well as other lovely hotels, rustic inns, trails, beaches, parks, boutiques, and the fort on the island.

Lesson: Take time to enjoy God's creation.

Both the Ford and Lutke families also explored Traverse City, Charlevoix, and Petoskey. On a longer trip, my family crossed the Mackinac Bridge and traveled in the Upper

Peninsula to observe the Soo Locks and other sights before exploring Canada, Michigan's northern neighbor.

Michigan touches four of the Great Lakes. Lake Michigan—the Big Lake—is located on the western shore where Carol and I live. Lake Superior borders Canada and Michigan to the north, while Lake Huron and Lake Erie are on Michigan's eastern shore, closer to the thumb area and below.

One need not travel very far to enjoy more than 11,000 pristine inland lakes, in addition to rivers and ponds. Locals and tourists enjoy boating, fishing, hunting, camping, golfing, snowmobiling, downhill skiing, and cross-country skiing. These are just a few of the activities available in Pure Michigan.

Carol and I feel fortunate to have been planted, to have grown strong roots, and to have blossomed in the "Mitten State."

Forever Friends Piece

A Fun Memory: Sharon (Kiel) VandeGevel

It must have been well after midnight because it had been dark for a long time. The night was clear and balmy. It was a great summer night for the Draco Horizon girls' slumber party.

As things go with silly teenagers at slumber parties, we planned to do something silly. It couldn't be just a fun night of games, telephone pranks, or normal mischief. No way! It happened that Doug, Carol's boyfriend, left his shiny black 1954 Ford convertible parked in the driveway waiting for the girls to take the car for a spin. Adventure was beckoning.

Six or maybe seven of the Draco Drips crowded into Doug's convertible. After putting the top down, off we went with the wind blowing through our hair. As young, fearless girls, fun was our goal. Anyway, life was good, and we thought we were pretty cool stuff. Actually, make that mighty cool stuff.

There was only one tiny problem. To drive this gorgeous automobile, one had to use the dreaded stick shift. When the road was smooth and flat, all was well. None of the Drips worried one second about Carol's inexperience with a stick shift.

We were headed downtown to cruise the circuit. The main part of this drive was a geographical square bordered by four streets that surrounded Veterans' Memorial Park in downtown Grand Rapids. If high school students had access to a car on a weekend evening, they would probably head for the downtown circuit because this was where all the cool teens went to flirt with members of the opposite sex. This was considered the weekend gathering spot for teens in the greater Grand Rapids area. And this was where the boys were.

I don't remember what happened between the square and Michigan Street hill, but evidently Carol wasn't trying to head home, because home would have been in the opposite direction. But even though we weren't speeding or running traffic signals, a police officer pulled over the convertible at the bottom of the hill. Talk about a spoilsport!

"Do you know what time it is?" the officer asked.

Well of course we knew what time it was. Not really. Sometime after midnight rings a memory bell.

After reminding the scared girls that it was after curfew and that nothing good happens this late, he told us that just a few blocks from this spot, there had been a robbery, and someone had been stabbed. We were shaking from fright at the thought of this.

After hearing that, we were smart enough to hightail it for home. There was only one little problem—the stick shift. Carol started the car, engaged the clutch, and put the shift into first gear, the proper way to go. However, when it came time to let out the clutch and give the car some gas to head up the hill, things took a turn for the worse. Did it help that the cop was watching? NO! Did it help that Carol's friends were yelling at her? Not really. In the 1950s it took far less to frighten a teenage girl than it does today, and believe me, Carol was scared. The tears were starting to flow, and she was having a tough time shifting gears.

The car was lurching and stalling, lurching and stalling, the transmission nearly hitting the ground. It seemed to take an eternity, but eventually the car started running almost smoothly. We all had been shouting at Carol to depress the clutch, so she did. Now the car was only a step up from idle, and we were going nowhere fast. I reached over, grabbed the gear shift lever, and very calmly and quietly said, "Carol, please put the clutch in, give the engine some gas, and then shift into second gear." Carol, with tears rolling off the end of her chin, cried, "I can't!"

Ah, what a night and what a fun memory!

Sharon has been a special longtime friend. She is a good musician and singer, and always keeps the girls smiling. Sharon and her husband, Mel, have three children and only one granddaughter, who is the apple of their eye. Sharon has served on the class reunion committee for years and is always a willing helper. Both Sharon and Mel have experienced some health issues, but after tests, surgery, and radiation, they are presently doing quite well.

CHAPTER TEN

the 1960s and 1970s

Community College

Carol and I made the decision to attend Grand Rapids Junior College after graduation from high school, and we worked at our summer jobs. Carol worked at a local fast-food restaurant on Twenty-Eighth Street, and I worked at the telephone company as a switchboard operator.

Although GRJC is now known as Grand Rapids Community College, it was conveniently located in downtown Grand Rapids, and Carol and I would ride to class with our Draco friend, Barb.

It wasn't until we registered for our classes and started communicating about what associate degree we wanted to obtain, that we actually got serious about being college students.

Barb and I were going into education, so we took our basic core classes. We started to get into the college mode, and we began meeting new and interesting students. In fact, I met Mary Leslee while registering for classes. She has always been known as "Rusty," because of her hair color.

Little did I know that Rusty's and my instant friendship would become a longtime relationship. We still often talk on the phone and visit whenever possible. Although she lives on the east side of the state in Clarkston, we talk regularly. My children call her Aunt Rusty, and I am known as Auntie Mare to her daughter, Leslee.

We Draco girls shared our many plans on the way downtown as we traveled to college. We were busy young ladies with college classes, activities, jobs, and dating lives, so the moments we spent together were precious.

First Marriages

I had been dating Wayne (Rip) Ripperda since my senior year in high school. He had graduated from Lee High School two years ahead of me, and he worked as an apprentice at General Motors while taking college classes, which continued into a thirty-five-year career at General Motors.

After he picked me up from work in the early evenings, we would get a bite to eat, go to a movie, or double date with couple friends. Late in the evening or extra early in the morning, I would study. I had little time for myself during those years because of having an extremely busy schedule.

Carol went on an eastern European tour with a college group the summer after her freshman year. She decided not to return to college the following September. Instead, she chose to work in the banking business. She later became engaged to a friend from Big Rapids whom she had known for years. After their marriage, she and her husband lived on the far south side of Grand Rapids.

During that time, Carol and I saw little of each other after she married, but we often talked on the phone. I was busy attending college, working, and dating Wayne, and I went away to attend Western Michigan University in the fall of my junior year.

Most of the Draco girls were married by the mid-to-late 1960s. We still tried to get together, although our schedules were diverse and busy. We continued to go to luncheons, see each other at five-year class reunions, and sometimes for other social activities.

The closeness the group had cultivated at Lee School never left us. Even to this day, we see each other several times a year. The women continue to enjoy a close relationship as most of us live in the Grand Rapids suburbs. This covers a distance from southeast Cascade to the southwest Hudsonville area, a distance of approximately thirty miles, which takes one-half hour of travel time.

Wayne and I became engaged, married in June of 1963, purchased a home in the suburb of Wyoming, which was close to our jobs, and enjoyed boating and traveling before starting a family. I was employed in human resources at a large food distribution company for three years. During that time, Carol continued working at a bank, and we saw each other occasionally.

Carol wanted to start a family, and when she later told me that she was pregnant, I hosted a baby shower for her just weeks before the child was due. The LHS girls attended, and we were excited to be together as a group. A few weeks later, we were deeply

Marilyn and Wayne's wedding, 1963

saddened to learn that Carol had delivered a stillborn baby boy. It was a difficult time for her, and eventually Carol and her husband divorced.

After I lost my first pregnancy in the second trimester, Carol and I met and discussed how disappointed we were. There were no formal support groups to lean on in these tragic situations. Generally, people didn't seem to discuss such things. Much has changed for the better over the years.

When Carol and I did talk on the phone or meet for lunch, it was as if nothing had changed. We still would converse for hours, even though weeks or months had passed. We never skipped a beat. New friends entered our lives, but our old friends were always there for us, even though most of the LHS girls were now married and starting families.

Carol lived with her parents for a few months after her divorce, and then shared an apartment with Dort, a friend who worked with her at the bank. They became good friends and were both single for five years between marriages.

Fortunately, I was able to get pregnant again, and Wayne and I had our first child, a daughter, Brenda (Bren), who was born in 1968. We were excited to welcome our first child into the family. Bren was the first grandchild on the Lutke side of the family.

Lesson: A family brings happiness and many blessings.

Reflecting

Looking back, the 1960s had been a difficult time for our country. President John F. Kennedy was assassinated in 1963, and the Vietnam War was in progress. The Detroit race riots occurred in 1967, and in 1968 Martin Luther King, Jr. and Robert Kennedy were assassinated.

However, the NASA Space Program thrilled America. There were many firsts, such as the first American to fly in space in 1961, the first American to circle the earth in 1962, and the first human to walk on the moon in 1969. Orbital flights, moon walks, and other achievements in space took place during the sixties and put a new adventurous spirit in the hearts of Americans.

Moving Forward

It was refreshing to be moving on to a new decade. In 1970 our second child, Todd, was born, and a few months later Wayne and I moved with our family to Cascade Township. Our new home was constructed in southeast Grand Rapids, and we continued living there for many years.

Life was enjoyable and busy for the Ripperda family, complete with a daughter and a son. I loved being a wife and a stay-at-home mother of two children. However, I knew that I would eventually return to college to finish the K-12 education degree which I had started in 1960.

One day in the early 1970s, Carol phoned, and I could tell by the excitement in her voice that she had wonderful news to share. Over lunch, she told me that Chuck Jennings, a man she had been dating for some time, had proposed to her. Carol had previously worked with him, and the love she had for Chuck was more than evident in her enormous smile and the glow on her face.

"There is something we need to talk about, though," Carol said hesitantly. "Chuck is divorced and has custody of his three sons, ages ten, eight, and four years old."

She looked at me with her big, expressive eyes and waited. I could read her body language. It was almost as if she was seeking my approval. Although I hadn't met Chuck, I knew Carol had been single for five years and had done some dating. I was sure she knew her own heart and had already decided to marry him.

"I want to be Chuck's wife, but do you think I will be a good stepmother to the boys? This is a package deal, Marilyn." Carol patiently awaited my comment.

"Of course, you will be a loving wife to Chuck and a wonderful stepmother to Chuck's sons.

The Jennings wedding, 1971

Because you love him, you will do a terrific job of mothering his children." I meant that, and I knew it was important for her to hear my sincere words.

Carol said that the boys' blood mother resided in another state. She would see the boys on school breaks and for a couple of weeks each summer. That would give Carol and Chuck time to be alone as well. There was a pause as we both sat pondering the situation. At that point Carol asked, "Do you think it will work, Marilyn?"

I assured her again that I thought her marriage would work because she loved Chuck. She would strive to be a good stepmother to his sons. I continued, "It will work out because you want your marriage to be successful. Give it your all, Carol, and God will bless your marriage."

Carol and Chuck married in 1971, and fifty years later, I still remember that conversation. Their marriage has been a loving and solid partnership. In fact, the blood mother passed away several years ago, and Carol has not only become the boys' mother and a mother-in-law to their wives, but she is a devoted grandmother to eight beautiful grandchildren as well.

Continuing Education

Another momentous conversation took place in the mid-seventies when something new and challenging was happening in Carol's life. She wanted to share the news with me in person.

"Marilyn, all three of our boys are in school, and I have been admitted to Aquinas College to attend the new Encore Program for returning adult students. I want you to consider finishing your few college credits, and perhaps we can graduate from college together."

Carol's eyes sparkled. I knew she was having a difficult time containing her excitement. She also seemed to know that I was ready to finish my college degree.

Aquinas College Graduation

Fast forward, I counseled with Aquinas College and took some education classes. After delivering a healthy baby girl, Tara Lyn, in 1976, I slowly finished two K-12 student teaching internships while Carol was completing her coursework in business.

We graduated together from Aquinas College in 1978, and our parents, husbands, children, and some of my siblings attended the ceremony. Carol and I were much more mature than we had been at our high school graduation in 1960.

Careers

Carol started working full time at Davenport College in 1979, and she traveled to Michigan high schools to recruit students. Later, she accepted a promotion as a placement adviser and guided students regarding curriculum matters. After working in academia for ten years, Carol started working part time in a bookstore in Grand Haven where she and Chuck then resided.

While Tara was in preschool, I substitute taught in area schools and then worked as a full-time high school English instructor. When Tara was in school, I became a K-12 reading consultant at several schools, where I tested, diagnosed, and taught. Later, I was a coordinator in a gifted and talented program, a computer consultant, and finally a language arts curriculum specialist in the Grand Rapids Public School District.

During these busy years, Carol and I would talk on the phone and meet for lunch, especially in the summer months when we had more time to chat and to catch up on our lives. We also enjoyed playing tennis and bridge, and we met for the annual luncheon with "The Ten."

Forever Friendship Piece

This I Remember: Nancy (Herbig) Greenwold

When I think back to my days at Lee High School and to the friendships I had, I recall wholesome fun, lots of laughter, and a deep sense of belonging and community. I have only positive memories of life in the Grand Rapids community during my first eighteen years. That is pretty amazing. I don't remember disagreements or anger or meanness, although there may have been some. I have a sense of growing up in a community where all adults cared for each other's children, where young people knew the behavior expected of them and were compliant most of the time. Except for the time when Donna Baar took the Draco girls for a joy ride in her dad's chicken truck before she was old enough to have a driver's license.

The families of the girls in our group differed in religion, beliefs, and income, but everyone respected and accepted each other and treated one another with dignity. We still do to this day. I think that is why we have maintained extra-close friendships for more than fifty-five years. We have accepted and affirmed each other exactly as we are which has allowed relationships to remain strong. I always know that I will be welcomed back by friends whenever I return to Michigan for a visit. When the girls get together, it is like we have never been apart. Our friendship picks up just like it was before.

I am so glad to have grown up in the Lee High School community, which grounded me in strong values that have stayed with me throughout my life. My early years there set the pattern for establishing caring, close relationships, as my family moved around the country. I have always had a sense of being rooted and secure because I belonged to a positive, supportive community in my growing-up years. The friendships I made at Lee High School provided a solid foundation that got me off to a good start in my life and continue to help me today.

Nancy married Doug, a classmate, and they have attended class reunions and other special occasions in Grand Rapids over the years. Nancy still lives in Maryland where two of her children and her grandchildren reside. Her son lives in Texas. Although Nancy still lives a distance away, she joins the group in Michigan whenever possible, and is still our sister. Today, she is an active widow.

CHAPTER ELEVEN

life goes on

Our Children

The Jennings' boys (David, Scott, and Mark) attended East Grand Rapids High School and graduated in the 1980s. Later, all three boys eventually graduated from Michigan State University, the alma mater of their father, Chuck, and their grandmother, Biddy. Now their grandchildren have graduated from MSU, with the exception of their youngest grandson, who is a senior. What a legacy for the family. Many additional family members are sure to be MSU Spartans. GO GREEN! GO WHITE!

Our daughter, Brenda, attended Michigan State University and Aquinas College. Her husband, Dean, attended Western Michigan University, and three of their children have graduated from Aquinas College and two are married. Their fourth child will also attend Aquinas. Their youngest son is in middle school. Their growing family is busy with sports activities, family travels, and visits to the Lake Leelanau cottage.

Todd, our son, met his wife, Kareen, at Michigan State University, where they both graduated. They now make South Carolina their home where they live with their family.

Three of their children now attend Clemson University. Their youngest son is in middle school. The Ripperda family stays active with sports, travel, boating, and enjoying a second home they purchased on a lake, with acreage.

Tara, our youngest daughter, is married to Nick, and they have a son in high school and a daughter in middle school. Both Tara and Nick graduated from the Forest Hills Public Schools where their children now attend and are active in sports.

After graduating from Grand Valley State University, Tara later received a nursing degree from Davenport University. Nick is a University of Michigan graduate, who also holds a law degree from Loyola University.

Both Tara and Nick are employed and live and work in the Grand Rapids area. They travel, are actively involved in their children's lives, including sports, and like all members of the greater family, enjoy visiting the family summer home on Lake Leelanau in the summer and fall months.

Wayne's Death

Never did our family imagine that in 1994, my husband, my children's father, Wayne, would suddenly pass away. Even now, twenty-nine years later, it is difficult to explain the loss that our family suffered when at the age of fifty-three, Wayne was called to his eternal home. He had a massive heart attack, coronary bypass surgery, rehabilitation, and suddenly passed away three weeks later from a pulmonary embolism.

Wayne and I had been married for thirty years, and life was busy with raising three children.

He always owned a boat and pulled many youngsters as he taught them to waterski. Coaching our children's youth sports teams and helping middle and high school teams as a parent assistant were his favorite pastime choices.

At the time of his death, he was called "Track Dad" as he coached Tara's girls' track team as an assistant. After working his regular job at General Motors, Wayne would rush to the football and baseball fields, or to the track to serve as a coach or an assistant to the coach. Because of his love of sports, he was available to serve youth in athletics.

He had been on football, track, and tennis teams in high school and still thrived on athletics in adulthood. He played tennis, golfed, enjoyed both water and snow skiing, and hunted and fished.

Wayne was active in our church as a deacon, and he enjoyed coaching the men's softball team. His weekends were often spent attending high school, college, and pro athletic games in the State of Michigan. Many times, Wayne would pile dads and their sons into our suburban or minivan, and they would drive to Lansing or Detroit to experience football or basketball finals.

As Wayne was recuperating in the hospital, he insisted that I follow Tara's track meet schedule to cheer her on. Days after his funeral, the family members made themselves available to support Tara's girls' relay team at the State of Michigan finals. Although it was difficult timing to attend this event, her family knew it would have been ultra-important for their dad to support his children in their sports endeavors. The Ripperda family was there together that day for Tara.

Although Wayne's death was devastating, it was a blessing that he didn't suffer for years. He left a legacy for his children. By being a loving, supportive husband and father, he is still missed immensely. But memories of him will forever be remembered by our family and close friendship circle.

The memories I hold dear even years later are the family times we spent together—meals, prayers, devotions, attending church as a family, sports events, plays, movies, going on trips to Disney World, Cancun, Mexico, the Upper Peninsula of Michigan, Chicago Cubs games, theme parks, camping, boating, skiing, and visits to our cottage as a family.

I am often asked how I survived such a shock. I answer that it was difficult. I grieved for several years and was happy for my family connections, my greater family, and for the friends and neighbors whom I have held dear over the years.

My church was wonderful to me. My involvement included becoming the chairperson of the elders and being on both the church board and the executive boards of my church.

It also helped that I had a busy career in education, and when Tara went away to college, I had more time to devote to my job. I also had time to travel with family and friends and learned how to become single again after a long marriage.

Leaving a Legacy

A special lake property that Wayne and I had purchased became our summer home on Leelanau Peninsula in northern Michigan. We had only four years of using the cottage before his death.

The Traverse City area of northern Michigan was a special place for the Ripperda family.

We had searched for six years with real estate agents to find the right summer home for our family.

In 1990, Wayne and I met with our real estate agent to view a property which had the ideal lakefront setting. However, we knew the smaller cabin would have to be replaced when our children married and grandchildren came along.

We made the decision to purchase the property and decorated the small cottage, making it our summer home. We had a dock out front with our ski boat, a fishing boat, and additional water toys.

One Christmas was spent up north ice skating on the lake and snow skiing in the area. Those precious memories can never be taken from our family.

Our Family Expands

Brenda, our oldest child, married Dean in 1992, and her father gave her away in marriage. It was a family affair with her sister, Tara, as the maid of honor, and her brother, Todd, served as a groomsman. Multiple friends were part of the wedding party, and Bren's Aunt Marcia and Uncle Jim served as mistress and master of ceremonies.

It was convenient that Bren and Dean lived and worked in Grand Rapids. They were available for family functions which included joining the family at the cottage.

After Todd's graduation from college, he chose to move to Chicago for his first job in the field of marketing and advertising.

Wayne didn't deal well with the fact that his son moved to another state, but Todd came home often and visited up north at the cottage. He especially spent time with the family in the summer months when it was possible to travel from Illinois.

Tara was in high school, and she and I would move north to the cottage in the summer months. Since I was an educator, we both had two months free to spend time in the Leelanau Peninsula of Michigan.

Together we found much peace on Lake Leelanau. Tara worked in Fishtown in the tourist town of Leland, a historical fishing village with shops and eateries. I hosted family and friends at our lake home and tended my flowers. In the meantime, I was busy making plans to expand our summer home.

After Wayne's death, the loneliness was more than I thought I could bear, but the peace my family and I received at the lake helped us during our grieving years.

My parents were still alive. They, my siblings, and close friends would often call and also visit me both at home and up north at our summer home.

Brenda and Dean had our first granddaughter, Morgan, just five months after Wayne's death.

Even though Wayne never got to see or hold any of our grandchildren, the entire family still enjoys being together. We try to meet as a group at the larger rebuilt cottage. Our children and grandchildren enjoy our summer home, and they think of it as a legacy to be passed down for generations to come.

Waterskiing, wakeboarding, fishing, boating, campfires, and diving for crawfish are favorite activities which the family enjoys on Lake Leelanau. Many pleasurable hours have been spent together at the family lake home over the years.

Moving On

During the years of grieving, I joined a singles group at church, a widowed persons group, played bridge, did line dancing, and volunteered. Another widow and I started a book club for single women, and I organized a single women's stock group for my friends who were interested in investments.

In addition, my girlfriends from high school, special neighbors, and friends from work kept me busy as well.

Finding other widows my age was helpful, and I made some close friendships during those years of widowhood. One friend in particular was dear to me because she lost her husband just months before Wayne died, and she and I attended many single functions together.

We both had three children, years later remarried, and now we have blended families with many grandchildren.

Being a widow for several years has given me empathy for new widows, and I try to spend time showing others that I care.

Chuck Jennings' Diagnosis

Shortly after Wayne's funeral, Chuck Jennings received a diagnosis of cancer. He went to the Mayo Clinic in Rochester, Minnesota for surgery to remove his prostate.

Carol and I often conversed, as both of us felt vulnerable, and we were extremely weary at that time. I was a widow and Carol had great anxiety.

Not only was Chuck recuperating from surgery, but Carol's mother, Mrs. Ford, a widow, was diagnosed with kidney disease around the same time. Carol feared losing both her husband and her mother. This was a difficult time in her life.

Carol's father had died from heart failure years before, and this diagnosis was a shock for Carol and her mother. Carol had been particularly close with her father and missed him very much. Now she, as an only child, was guiding her mother in decision-making regarding selling her home, transporting her to kidney dialysis treatments, and gradually moving her to a senior living home before her death.

Chuck returned to his job until 1997, where he was a senior vice president and director of human resources at the former Old Kent Financial Corporation. He had spent his entire career working at the bank.

Retirement

Upon Chuck's retirement, Carol also retired from The Bookman, a job Carol enjoyed at a local Grand Haven bookstore where she had met many interesting people.

Following Carol and Chuck's retirement and Mrs. Ford's death, the Jennings family, complete with their three sons, their wives, and five grandchildren, flew to Mexico for a family vacation. After returning from their Mexico trip, Carol and Chuck sold their home on Spring Lake. They purchased a condominium in the Village of Spring Lake located on the Grand River near Grand Haven and Lake Michigan.

Forever Friends Piece:

Best Friends Forever – Judy (Geelhoed) Walkotten

What a ton of great memories I have with all the Draco Drips. Let's start with birthday parties at each girl's home and slumber parties at Carol's house. Add to that the great time at the Eagle's Nest cottage in Grand Haven. Since most of the group was in band, we share many great memories of band camp and of marching in the Red Flannel Days and Santa Parades, at football games, the Holland Tulip Festival, and the University of Michigan halftime show on Band Day. What fun memories! The band bus trips were particularly memorable with everyone singing, joking, and eventually napping as the bus neared home.

Along with those happy times, we are there for each other in sad times. As a group we mourned the loss of our parents and of a spouse, Marilyn's dear first husband, Wayne. Then we experienced the death of one our own, the first of "The Ten," when Marcia passed away after a courageous battle with cancer.

I hope and pray that the Draco girls will spend many more wonderful times together as we age.

Judy became a good friend, and we spent much time together babysitting, double-dating, and participating in each other's weddings. Judy and her husband, Rich, have four children and several grandchildren and great-grandchildren living in Michigan. For many years, Judy and Rich spent the winter months in Arizona in their early retirement years. Judy is quite healthy and is the caretaker for her husband, who is presently having some health difficulties. We pray for both Judy and Rich.

CHAPTER TWELVE

happiness again

Travel Plans

After retirement from my career in education in 2002, I started planning a trip. So much had happened since the death of my husband, and then my mother passed away from cancer in 2001.

I took my first European trip with my work friend, Sue Ellyn, one year after Wayne's death. We went with a group from Calvin College (now University) and enjoyed a wonderful trip as part of an eastern European experience. Visits to Berlin and other countries including Poland, Hungary, Slovakia, and Czech Republic were part of our itinerary.

Since then, I enjoyed several ocean cruises and many trips to Florida and Mexico. My next destination was in question when I spoke with my older sister, Joanie. She suggested a family trip with Dad, who was a new widower, David, her husband, and her. The four of us planned to start the trip together, and then I would travel independently.

We decided that Arizona would be a nice place to escape to in January. We began to make plans and were off on an airplane to Phoenix, Arizona, to explore Sedona and the Grand

Canyon. The four of us stayed at a lodge at the Grand Canyon, hiked, and explored the beautiful country.

After renting a car and driving to San Diego, we visited my father's youngest sister, our Aunt Ruth. We stayed with her, toured the area, and she served as our guide.

My father, Joanie, and David flew back to Michigan, while I flew to Las Vegas to visit with my former neighbor, Marlene, for one month at her home in a community which was just miles from the strip.

Then I flew to Florida and stayed with longtime friends, Marie and Tom O'Hara, in Bradenton. Upon renting a car, I drove to visit Carol and Chuck at their home in Naples. This was one of my favorite areas of Naples, close to Marco Island where I had vacationed years before with my family.

Carol and I had a great time catching up, shopping, eating at restaurants on Marco Bay, and exploring Marco Island and Naples. Chuck took us out for a wonderful dinner. We then explored Fifth Avenue.

My final destination was to meet three of my book club friends, Nancy, Suzanne, and Sue Ellyn, on Fort Myers Beach. I rented a car and met the girls for a delightful week of shopping, going to the beach, and dining out. Then I needed to fly home to file my income tax returns.

A Special Phone Call

As I parked my car and approached my condo in Caledonia, I could hear the phone ringing.

Thinking it was a family member, I nearly broke my neck answering that call.

A gentleman, Art Emery, was calling from the east side of Michigan. A mutual friend had given him my phone number. His voice sounded very inviting.

Out of breath, I asked him to wait for one minute while I carried my luggage inside. I had left my belongings outside, as I had scurried to answer the phone call.

Upon conversing for several minutes, I learned that Art had been widowed for twelve years and had recently retired from a business career in the Detroit suburbs.

Art had raised two daughters alone, and they were now attending college. When he told me his age, that he was a Christian, and had been in the military as a Marine, plus he had earned a master's degree, I knew that this was an interesting man and someone I would eventually like to meet.

After several weeks of communicating via phone and email, we arranged a coffee date when he would be in Grand Rapids seeking an apartment for his daughter, Tiffany. She had enrolled at Grand Valley State University at the nearby campus and would be starting college in the fall. His oldest daughter, Allison, was a student at the University of Houston.

The coffee date was successful, and we found through conversation that we had mutual friends living in Grand Rapids. Art had visited western Michigan in the past and was interested in learning more about the city where I had been born, educated, and still had a home.

When we met, I had been a widow for nine years and was a grandmother to five grandchildren. As a recent retiree, the Kent Intermediate School District asked me to give occasional educational presentations. My availability was in the spring and fall months, because my summer months were spent at my cottage in northern Michigan, and I took trips to Florida in the winter to friends at various locations in the Sunshine State.

I learned that Art was born and raised in Detroit, Michigan, and had worked as a director of labor relations at General Dynamics, a Fortune 500 Company located in the Detroit suburb of Sterling Heights. Also, he enjoyed traveling. Some months later, I learned that he was a very organized and detailed person.

Art has a love for God, his family, and his country. His friendship base is important to him.

We agreed on many of the same issues and had similar tastes.

Although we both had dated others over the years, neither Art nor I were in a rush to remarry at this point in our lives. That took the pressure off. We focused on having fun as we learned to know each other better. It was apparent that we had many of the same interests. We eventually met each other's family and friends, who were important people in our lives.

Wedding Plans

Art and I dated for a year and a half, fell in love, became engaged, and made plans to marry in November 2004. There is no doubt the Lord brought us together because we were not looking for a serious relationship prior to meeting each other.

After setting a date and deciding on the Cascade Christian Chapel for our wedding ceremony, we reserved a room at a nearby Crowne Plaza Hotel for our Saturday reception and a Sunday brunch. The chapel and hotel were close to the expressway for traveling guests.

We made plans for my father and my son, Todd, to walk me down the aisle, and to give me away at Art's and my impending wedding ceremony. We were excited while making plans for our marriage and our future together.

When I called Carol to invite her to stand by my side as my matron of honor, she accepted my invitation through tears.

"Yes, I will be there at your side, Marilyn." Carol said that she and Chuck would make plans to fly to Grand Rapids from Florida early, so she and I would have time for lunch and to get a beauty treatment together before the wedding. She thanked me for asking her and was happy to fly home for our wedding and reception.

We had a lovely wedding with family and close friends on a cold November evening in Cascade. Our five children, their mates/dates, and my five grandchildren helped us celebrate. In addition, two of my aunts (one from California), and Art's uncle and cousin from Pennsylvania, and many friends of ours from Grand Rapids, and the Detroit suburbs were in attendance.

Following the reception and brunch the next morning, Art and I—Mr. and Mrs. Art Emery— spent our honeymoon in Florida. We returned to Art's home in Sterling Heights, where we lived and prepared to sell his house in the spring.

The Emery wedding, 2004

Lesson: Never forget to thank God
for the joy of family.

Our Family

Art and I purchased a home in Cascade, in western Michigan, where we moved and have been living for the past several years. Two of our children still live in the suburbs of Grand Rapids, and now we have three families who live elsewhere: South Carolina and Texas.

Our blended family has grown to fifteen grandchildren to date, and a great-grandson, Asher Alan, was born in 2020.

In addition to spending many holidays and birthday celebrations together, our family celebrates high school and college graduations. We held a family reunion in the summer of 2019 on Mackinac Island.

Most holidays have been spent at Art's and my Grand Rapids home, but now the children are hosting gatherings at their homes as well. The family has shared showers, weddings, births, baptisms, confirmations, and special anniversaries over the years where family pictures are taken.

This past Thanksgiving, the family traveled to South Carolina to celebrate Art's and Marilyn's eightieth birthdays on Johns Island.

CHAPTER THIRTEEN

a tribute to marcia

Diagnosis

Marcia (Van Till) Stuit, our Draco sister and forever friend, was diagnosed with stage four cancer in November 2010. She attended the December Christmas luncheon and shared an emotional time with the Draco women.

The following May, Carol and I went to lunch with Marcia and Donna (another Draco sister).

I asked Marcia if she would feel comfortable penning a journal of her journey. I explained that Carol and I were writing a book about our longtime friendship and that the group of ten LHS girls and the class of 1960 would be included in the book.

I said, "The girls would cherish a copy of your journal, and if you decide to write a piece, it would be included in a chapter of the book." In addition, I stressed that there would be no rush or pressure, just a few words from her heart were what Carol and I desired.

Marcia smiled and promised that she would try her best to write a journal while feeling well. Later, a handwritten journal was mailed to me. I profoundly thanked her just months before she passed away in November of 2012.

Marcia's Journal

How can I put into words how I felt as nine of my dear friends laid their hands on me and prayed heartfelt blessings? This occurred at Sue's home where the girls gathered for an annual Christmas luncheon, one I usually miss, as Mel, my husband, and I are in Florida for the winter months.

But this year we are back in Michigan and I'm facing the fight of my life. We had been in Florida just one week when a very swollen left ankle brought me to the hospital. A blood clot was found near that ankle. The plan was blood thinners, bed rest, elevation of the leg, and then discharge.

Next, there were blood tests, a liver biopsy, and a scope of my esophagus.

The day before Thanksgiving, I was alone in the hospital room when the doctor came in and bluntly told me, "You should go home and enjoy your children. You have metastatic carcinoma of your esophagus."

Good thing I was lying down when he added, "You probably have six months to live. I'm sorry." And with that, he left me.

Did he really say these things? How could Miss Independent, always healthy and strong, be hearing such a pronouncement? I kept saying, "If I didn't know I had cancer, I wouldn't know I had cancer."

With my leg stretched out, we left Florida for home two weeks after we arrived. I told my dear husband, "You're going to have to drive faster than usual, because we need to bring my medical records to our doctor's appointment at 10:15 a.m. Wednesday."

Mel had to give me an anticoagulant shot every twenty-four hours. (Nurse Marcia couldn't give it to herself!) Mel, who had never given an injection even to an animal, became a very proficient nurse. This ritual continued even after we were home for several days.

Friday, I sat across from my oncologist at Lacks Cancer Center in Grand Rapids. He looked over my records and certainly didn't talk very optimistically. Our children, Michelle and Mike, were at the appointment with us to take notes. Mel and I were on brain overload and had trouble recalling all the information that had lately come our way.

I pointed up to the ceiling and said, "I've got a pipeline to heaven. The Great Physician can heal me if it's His will." And I believe that with all my heart. I'm on numerous prayer chains, and even complete strangers say they'll be praying for me. Friends and church family members have been supportive in many ways, showing love and concern.

So far, I've had a series of six chemo treatments. They make for long days. (Four to five hours of chemo with more waiting time to get started and to draw labs.) Mel and I try to be patient. Because these drugs are strong, it's not unusual for a person's hemoglobin to drop, and I needed two units of blood near the end of the six treatments. This was very upsetting news. I cried much of the time during chemo sessions. *I've always been so healthy, Lord. What's happening to me?*

It's a rather scary time, but I must keep trusting. For a Christian, getting through this cancer walk is a win-win situation. It will be either remission, a cure, or eternity with my Lord and Savior.

February 2, 2012: I had new chemo treatments over three hours, and I was home with an infusion pump going for the next forty-six hours. The pump was carried in a fanny pack. Then the same routine took place again after two weeks followed by two weeks off. Twenty-four hours into the process, I was doing okay.

Now, on a happier note, as I've been writing about my walk with cancer, I've been thinking about the "why" of an almost lifelong connection with nine girlfriends. Lee School was the center of our existence once we were there. Depending on where we'd lived prior to Lee or Godfrey schools, we all got together in the eighth grade at Lee, and most of our relationships and our real fun began then.

Marcia Passed Away November 27, 2012

After Marcia's death, I was invited to present a eulogy at her funeral. On the day of the funeral, the LHS sisters lined up in the back of the church and followed the casket up the center aisle. We sat as a group with our husbands in the sanctuary, and Marcia's nurse friends followed and sat as a group as well.

Lesson: Love your friends. When they are gone, there is a huge hole in your heart.

Eulogy by Marilyn Emery

When the Draco sisters turned forty years old, we began visiting at special places. Once we gathered in Grand Haven for a luncheon at Carol's condo overlooking Lake Michigan. Years later, we held a sleepover at Carol's Spring Lake home. For our fiftieth birthday celebration, we drove north to Ludington and spent the weekend at a bed and breakfast.

Our last overnight adventure took place at Lake Leelanau, with an outing at my summer home, when the girls turned sixty-five years old. There was talk about meeting in Florida in 2012, but those plans were canceled due to Marcia's health condition.

Upon learning of Marcia's passing, Pastor Dale Kronemeyer wrote, "Sure wish I could be at Marcia's funeral service, but we were in Michigan in September and there is much going on in Arizona right now. Please pass on my love to everyone, and I will keep my prayers going that Marcia's confidence of her heavenly home will have an influence on those who need to know our Lord."

Marcia attended our fifty-year class reunion in 2010, and she asked if she could present an overview of the journey our class had taken together over the years. The class had lost other classmates, but we didn't know that our fifty-year reunion would be Marcia's last time to meet with the class.

Fiftieth Birthday celebration in Ludington

We thank God for her life and celebrate the wonderful years that He gave to Marcia. We shall miss Marcia, her many talents, her happiness, and her courage.

The last time I saw Marcia and spoke with her was one week before her homegoing. A group of church friends and three of her longtime friends, Donna, Sharon, and I, met at Marcia's home where we sang some of her favorite hymns. Marcia clearly enjoyed the singing, and yet it was apparent that she was tired and longed for eternal rest.

The group prayed over Marcia after singing the last chorus of a hymn about meeting in heaven with rejoicing, singing, and shouting upon meeting our Savior face to face.

I left first and spoke to Marcia alone, saying softly, "Marcia, if I don't see you on earth, I shall see you in heaven."

In a clear voice she replied, "I'll be there to greet you, dear friend."

I kissed Marcia's forehead and left. Yes, I wept in the car as I sat alone and drove to an appointment.

Surely the Lord was present in Marcia's room. Being with our longtime friend was an honor for each person in attendance at her church service that day.

(*Marcia is our shining star in heaven awaiting each one of the nine sisters. Our group shall never forget our dear friend. Marcia's memory will be forever present whenever the group meets.*)

Forever Friendship Piece:

Friendship Sisters – Donna (Baar) Tillema

Barb and Jackie were my great friends, and we attended Godfrey Elementary School. My best friend, Marcia, attended Lee School, but we were always together because we lived nearby and attended the same church. Judy also went to our church.

Eventually, I met Sandy, who attended Lee School. She and Marcia were cousins. When the Godfrey students joined their Lee School classmates, I met Carol, Marilyn, Nancy, Sharon, and Sue since we all were members of the Horizon Club, which met at Barb's home.

I had fun in high school. I remember when I jumped out of a first-floor window in bookkeeping class. I walked to Sharon's house a few blocks away to get some money to buy donuts since it was donut day at school.

One April Fools' Day I left school as a prank, and I spent the next week in detention hall every afternoon after school.

In high school the girls were invited to my house to make pizza. They hopped on the back of my dad's flatbed truck so we could go shopping for hamburger meat. I didn't have a driver's license but had driven with my father before. No one saw us leave or return from the store.

Marcia, Barb, and I walked to the drugstore for Cherry Cokes after school almost every day.

Somehow that became a pattern.

I recall one Sunday night driving around the circuit in Grand Rapids with Sharon and Jackie. Another car with three students from different schools bumped into us. We stopped to talk with these guys, and I eventually ended up marrying one of them.

Marcia, Sharon, and I sang in a trio at special events. We sang at Sharon's mother's eightieth birthday party, at churches, and at several of our class reunions.

I thank God for this special group of sisters, and I pray for them daily.

Donna Baar is known as "Baarsie," the name our group gave her in high school. Besides making the girls smile, she has a huge heart. Donna makes delicious fudge, which she gives as gifts each Christmas. Twice a year our group picture arrives in the mail weeks after each event, compliments of Donna. Since Marcia was her best friend throughout life, Donna kept us updated on Marcia's health issues in the final year of our dear friend's life. Donna is a fine example of a loving and caring friend. Both Donna and her husband, Arn, have had some health issues the past few years. She has had some surgeries and Arn is currently on oxygen, yet they are still active. Recently, they moved into an independent senior living home near their family in a suburb of Grand Rapids.

CHAPTER FOURTEEN

classmate memories

A few additional classmates were invited to share articles for the book. Marty Reynolds came to Lee from Godwin School in the eighth grade, and it took him little time to become instant friends with several of his new classmates.

Marty lived in the Godfrey area, quickly acclimated to the surroundings, and became a neighbor and close friend of Bob Velding, another classmate. Both Marty and Bob played sports, and in their junior year, rode to school each day in Marty's purple 1953 Chevy.

One day Marty's car would not move forward when he put it into drive, but it moved in reverse gear. Of course, Marty picked up Bob as usual, and they drove one mile in reverse all the way to school. Somehow, they made it to school on time and even dodged the police on the way. Marty did get the transmission fixed shortly after this hilarious backward experience.

Carol: Marty Reynolds

This is how I remember Carol (Ford) Jennings. Thinking back to our Lee High School years, I recall that Carol was a little more devilish than the rest of the girls who ran around together. For example, rumor had it that she smoked in the girls' restroom.

Although she might have been a little mischievous, Carol always seemed to be there when you needed her. I never heard anyone say anything negative about her. I remember the parties at her house. It seemed like Carol would invite most of the kids from Lee High School after many football or basketball games.

I became closer to Carol after we graduated from high school, because we were on the committee working on the class reunions. The one thing that stands out for me about Carol is her lust for life. Through all the years we have been classmates, I have not seen her in a down mood. Even after her stroke, she remains the same devilish, fun-loving Carol I have known for sixty years.

Marty graciously hosts our class reunion committee and has kept our class connected for several years. He calls meetings, and plans are made by the committee of seven, who work together as a team. We start the planning process a year in advance for every five-year class reunion. Marty is in good health, and his wife, Lynda, and he have a winter residence in Florida where they enjoy boating. They have been married for forty-two years.

Lee High School Class of 1960 Memories: Pastor Dale Kronemeyer

Memories are such a great thing. They bring us back in a nostalgic way to some of the most important times from our past, times that have had a lifelong impact on us. Some of those memories you kind of wish were not there, because of the embarrassing nature of an event—like missing a kiss I was to plant on my stage wife "Madge"/Marcia in the senior play titled *The Unguided Miss,* which for me became more about the unguided kiss. Lesson learned. I should have spent a lot more time practicing that kiss.

Through the years at reunions and other gatherings, I would often greet dear Marcia by asking, "Well, how has my first wife been doing?" And then I suffered a broken heart many years later when talking with my Madge and praying with her as she was dealing with the news about the cancer that would soon claim her life.

The people who used to play together as kids continued to play, to love, to share, and even to pray with each other. We had so many memories from the most important years of our lives and we continued to build memories through the years as we gathered for LHS reunions.

> The people who used to play together as kids continued to play, to love, to share, and even to pray with each other.

Then many dear friends (Judy, Rich, Marilyn, Art, Bob, Sandy, Sue, Ron, Doug, Ruth, Tom, Bev) would make a point of visiting my wife, Mo, and me at our home in Arizona.

There was something unique about the LHS class of 1960, and special memories prompt classmates to spend time together even today. Who would have thought in 1960 at the completion of our senior year in high school, that fifty-five years later we would have such special relationships in our senior years?

Dale, a retired pastor still pastors a flock in Mesa, Arizona. He is also the technology representative of our class reunion committee. Dale and his wife, Mo, have had a few cancer scares. Dale recently finished radiation treatment. At this point, they are thankful to God for making such fine recoveries.

The Godfrey-Lee Community – A Convergence of Blessings: Doug Greenwold

I suspect most people tend to view their school years through rose-colored glasses. But when it comes to the Lee High School class of 1960, there were good reasons for viewing those years that way. Individually and collectively, we benefited from a convergence of community blessings. For friendships to take root and bloom and then to foster enduring memories, a nurturing soil is needed. That's what our Godfrey-Lee community blessed us with in southwest Grand Rapids.

While the class of 1960 was one of the largest classes in the history of LHS (eighty-two graduates), Godfrey-Lee was still considered a small community (approximately three hundred students in grades nine through twelve). That meant everyone was known in the classroom and in the community. Many of our parents graduated from LHS, which gave the community stability and continuity. As a result, our parents knew the other kids in our neighborhoods, which certainly kept a lid on any potential tomfoolery.

From a guy's perspective on the Godfrey side of the district, we were blessed with an idyllic neighborhood. There was Happy Hollow, a thirty-acre wild area with a pond (perfect for making Tom Sawyer rafts to float on an imaginary Mississippi), an abandoned railroad track, Plaster Creek, and several gentle treed hills and valleys just right for building camps and hideouts.

Next to Happy Hollow were the LHS athletic fields always ready to welcome yet another pickup game. Vacant lots on the streets were ideal for playing waffle ball and touch football and for building miniature golf courses. Throw in a gravel pit or two, and there was always something to occupy us. When winter came, we shoveled driveways and played one-on-one/two-on-two basketball games until the third call for supper. When it got really cold, we played hockey in a basement. Year-round sports were our oxygen. As a result, we developed into good athletes, which made for successful LHS teams.

We were blessed with a stable community made up of intact families. Divorce was a rarity. Churches were a prominent part of many families' lives. There was no crime and there were no safety concerns. We played games of kick-the-can in the street when the sun went down, and no one thought twice about that. Benign mischief was the worst problem adults had to deal with.

Sneaking into the JV football game to save a dime was a high crime. Being naughty was calling the coach, Mr. Wright, Uncle Louis behind his back.

In those days there was no such thing as political correctness. We were after all, the Lee Rebels. (I don't recall another team in Michigan with that name!)

Nutrition was not a notion in our world. To raise funds for student organizations, we sold donuts on a certain day and ice cream drumsticks on another. If PC meant anything, it was peaches and cream.

LHS benefited from this mosaic of community blessings, and its faculty enhanced it. We had excellent role models in Mr. Wright, Mr. Teusink, Mr. Post, and Mr. McKindley, who were all chosen by Reuben Young, our principal. Mr. Young was an ex-professional wrestler with a barrel chest and a look that could turn your resolve into melted butter. No one wanted to be the recipient of his gaze and certainly not of his iron-fisted grip. As a result, proper decorum was never an issue, and woe to the person who dared to cross Mr. Young's line.

In 1942 the community was blessed with a special group of war babies who would become the LHS class of 1960. The class was blessed with good students, leaders, and athletes. In 1960 our basketball team was number one in the state for most of the year, and our baseball team lost only one game. Add to that a marching band of eighty (twenty-five percent of the school population), that consistently won marching competition trophies. 1960 was a banner year chock-full of good outcomes and great memories. We were blessed but didn't know it until much later.

Such was the LHS community and therefore our high school world. While the rose-colored glasses may still be in place, it was indeed a special moment in time, and our shared experiences continue to serve as the glue of lifelong friendships and to preserve fond memories. We were the beneficiaries of a convergence of blessings.

Doug was our class valedictorian and a talented basketball and baseball player in high school. He held the honor of being in the LHS "Rebel Hall of Fame." Doug passed away in June 2019 and is sadly missed by his family, friends, and classmates.

CHAPTER FIFTEEN

mischief with friends

Our Word Was Our Bond

Carol's and my friendship from the beginning was trustworthy and kind. Even as elementary girls, we never interlocked pinkies nor professed to tell the truth on a stack of Bibles. There was no mention of being struck dead if we were caught breaking promises or telling lies. Making promises was not an integral part of our relationship. It was always an open and transparent acceptance of each other. We shared almost everything over the years, and we had few secrets from each other.

The Huge Scary Tree

Starting in middle school, Carol was in early morning choir, and I was in band, so we went our separate ways once we entered the building. We had some classes together and then met for lunch with the Draco girls and classmates in the lunchroom. It was a fun time to have others join us at noon.

If we went to the Dairy Bar as young girls or to Jeanette's Corner Store for treats, we'd shop, then walk down Chicago Drive to our block. As we walked, we'd eat our treats. Everything was cool, and there was lots of laughter and fun.

Carol would walk with me past five houses on our street, then we'd part ways at the halfway mark.

"Bye friend, see you tomorrow," we'd say as we parted.

If it was light outside, she'd walk back to her house on the corner, and I'd continue walking toward Engle Street to my family home in the middle of the block. However, if it was getting dark, we'd run home.

It was not because our neighborhood was unsafe, but because of the huge scary tree just doors from the Ford home. The sidewalk was built around this large, sprawling tree. We had to pass it to get to the middle mark, where we parted ways. Carol had to pass it twice! We imagined that the bogeyman was hiding behind that enormous ugly tree.

When we were in high school and prior to having driver's licenses, we would be out with groups for sporting events, skating parties in the old school gym, dances, and club functions. When we stopped at the Soda Bar for a snack or Cherry Coke after an event, we would walk as a group. Carol and I were the only two walking on Delwood Avenue; the others had dropped out to maneuver their way home.

> We chuckled at the memory but knew that a vow to save each other was like an unbroken promise.

When we got near the horrible tree, we'd run to our drop-off point. At night, there were only streetlights and dim lights visible from houses.

We'd say, "See you later, alligator," and then run like crazy to get home. Our vow was to yell if we needed help. Especially, Carol, who had to escape twice from the scary tree and hidden demons lurking nearby.

Recently, Carol and I did a Delwood tour to see our homes from the past. Lo and behold, the tree from our memories was no longer there. We assumed it had probably fallen or been chopped down years before. As adults, we laughed at all the grief that tree had caused us for multiple years.

"You know, Carol, I would wait by my house to make sure I didn't hear you yell for help."

Carol smiled and said, "I would run across neighbors' lawns or walk in the road to escape that awful tree."

We chuckled at the memory but knew that a vow to save each other was like an unbroken promise.

A Different Time

The 1950s and early 60s were post-World War II and quite a different time than today. Much was expected of us as children, youth, and young adults. However, we could be mischievous without being huge troublemakers.

We knew either our parents would find out or the school principal would call us into the office for any inappropriate actions. That meant being grounded at home or serving detention time at school. Carol and I wanted nothing to do with those consequences!

As youngsters, we basically stayed in our neighborhood. We played games such as hopscotch, "I send," tag, kick-the-can, softball, and boardgames with neighbor kids.

In middle school, we sometimes had babysitting jobs in our neighborhoods.

Driving Mischief

When one of us drove, we often crammed too many kids into our cars. We had bench front seats, so it was possible to stuff seven friends into an average-size car.

If a boyfriend was driving, the girlfriend would settle close beside him because bench seats allowed for that, and the boyfriend would drive with one arm wrapped around his girlfriend.

After he dropped her off at home, he would park in the driveway for some alone time. It was safer than parking other places. Our parents would turn the outdoor light off and on when it was time to end the date. At least, mine did.

The dollar-night drive-in theaters were always packed. We would sometimes hide kids in the trunk of our car to gain entry for them. Did we get caught? Yes, a few times. Of course, we would keep these events quiet.

Sometimes we threw our change together to pay for gas to drive to McDonald's for fifteen-cent hamburgers. There were times we had enough for fries and shakes too.

The fun was in being together as a group of girls—carefree and laughing.

Was it possible to meet boys while driving around with a group of girls? It surely was, especially at the beach, the Rainbow Grill, and Big Boy drive-up restaurants. We'd park our car, call in our order, eat in the car, and boys from other cars would visit us. As long as we stayed in a group, it was safe. In fact, one of our sisters met her husband that way. He called her, they dated, and married years later.

The One-Way Street

One evening Donna was driving a car full of girls near the Grand Rapids Public Library and Lincoln Park on a one-way street. She kept yelling at people to get into the proper lane. They yelled back telling her that she was in error. That was when she realized she had been driving the wrong way on a one-way street. As soon as she could, she turned the car around and sheepishly drove away.

T-Papering Incident

When Carol and the girls t-papered the car of an older student one night, he showed up in her driveway the next morning. He asked if she was out t-papering the night before and if she was responsible for the mess made of his car.

Carol confessed that she and her friends had indeed t-papered his car the night before.

He was insulted that he had to take it to a car wash to remove the paper stuck to the windows.

It had rained, and he couldn't clean the car himself.

Carol thought he wanted compensation for the car wash. Instead, he angrily drove off.

Did that curtail further t-paper decorating events? NO way! However, car windows were no longer the top priority after that incident.

Skating

Saturday night skating was a fun event for Lee High School students before they could drive. After a night of roller skating in the old gym, the couple would walk to the girl's house. The guy would carry the girl's skate case to her home and would expect a kiss at the back door.

If the couple was going steady, he would leave his case behind, carry his girlfriend's case, then circle back to get his case and go home. Sometimes the guys would meet at the local Fry House for a coke and burger on their way home.

As a rule, the boys were kind and respectful. If the couple liked each other, the girl was glad to be escorted home from roller skating. However, if she preferred to carry her own case home, it was an indication that she wasn't interested in the boy. No way was she going to give him a smooch at her back door!

Sex Education

Most of our mothers were the main source of learning about the birds and the bees. My older sister and my aunts also served as mentors for me. Moms gave their daughters a book to read about the facts of life when they were in their tweens. We asked questions but basically talked amongst ourselves with our girlfriends. The female gym teacher also instructed us in a very minor way.

Due to a close-knit family and community, there were people who cared about students and their upbringing. Relatives, school counselors, or teachers would be helpful if their advice was needed.

Although teens parked and made-out, very few girls became pregnant or married as teens.

The culture dictated that students were responsible for themselves and for making wise decisions.

Were we goody two-shoes? No, we were responsible young people. We knew there was more in life and that God had a purpose for our lives. We believed that good things would come in God's timing and in His way. We were willing to wait.

The Family in the 1950s and 60s

Families spent time together. The extended family would gather for the milestones of family members, such as birthdays, graduation, etc. Families enjoyed time as a group and often vacationed together.

Most individual families attended church on Sunday, and it was a quiet day of rest.

Groceries, gas, and most other shopping was done on Saturday. The Sunday focus was on God and going to church twice per day with a big family meal between services. The children and youth went to morning Sunday school and church. Then a youth group service was held before the evening service. There was an occasional hymn sing or a house gathering after the evening service.

Fathers worked during the week and did the yard work, painting, as well as maintaining the car. Most mothers were housewives. They cooked, cleaned, shopped, sewed, and attended school and women's meetings and various clubs.

There was a mid-week church prayer group. My father was also busy as the Sunday School Superintendent and an elder.

CHAPTER SIXTEEN

thelm and lou adventures

Northern Michigan Summer Adventures –
Straight-line Windstorm: Carol

Marilyn invited me to spend a few days up north at her cottage to work on the manuscript, and I decided that we'd call it our summer adventure. We planned to have fun reading the document and focus on finishing the last chapters of our journey.

Our plan was to go to our favorite restaurants and shops in Leland and Suttons Bay. If time allowed, the Sleeping Bear Dunes and shops in downtown Traverse City were on our list of things to do.

However, the weather changed drastically on Sunday, the day we arrived. When we pulled into the garage and unpacked the car, we noticed the sky was filled with dark clouds. A storm was brewing.

A mysterious gray haze appeared over the lake, and the sky continued to grow darker. The wind picked up. A pounding rain followed. Was a tornado developing?

As Marilyn was securing a shelter in the downstairs bathroom where we could hide away from windows, the electricity went out.

I yelled, "Marilyn, a tree is falling in the front yard. It's falling toward the lake!"

We watched the blue spruce spread its branches and gracefully fall to the ground. Branches, dirt, leaves, and other debris flew through the air. We stared in shock!

It wasn't a tornado, but a straight-line windstorm.

About twenty minutes later, the sky cleared, and the sun came out. We stepped outside to check the side of the house. Electrical lines were down, and dozens of massive trees were uprooted and lying across the driveway. The private road was not visible, much less the main road.

The scene was surreal. Did this really happen?

Marilyn's neighbor called out, asking if we were all right.

Marilyn hollered back, "We're fine. We can hear you, but we can't see you. Are the two of you alright?"

After yelling that they were fine, her neighbor said that due to fallen trees, it was impossible to check on the other two homeowners on the private road, which meant that the residents on the private road were isolated. The only way to leave this densely treed area was by boat.

As we walked around the cottage to inspect the outside of the structure, we started calling each other Thelm (Thelma) and Lou (Louise).

Later, when we discussed what had just happened, our primary focus was the blessing of being alive and of having a comfortable place to sit, eat, and sleep. Things could have been far worse if the trees had hit the cottage.

Walking out onto the dock, we discovered that a canoe had been thrust halfway off its wooden perch. Objects such as deck chairs and water toys from other homes were floating in the lake.

We felt trapped as we peered at the lake in front of the cottage and then the dense woods on both sides. With the huge trees that had fallen across the yard and the driveway, we were isolated from the outside world.

After dining on a salad and sandwiches, we realized that without electricity, the refrigerated foods would not stay cold for many days.

When the darkness of night descended upon the lake, we went upstairs with candles and the manuscript to go work at the desk. We still needed to write the final chapters of our book.

> When Marilyn and I discussed having an adventure, never could we have imagined experiencing a straight-line windstorm.

Even though the conditions weren't perfect, we concentrated and discussed the manuscript and made a few decisions. Occupying our time this way kept us from worrying about the mess outside. We had a goal in mind for the weekend, and sitting in the dark wasn't part of our weekend plan.

Finally, I took my candle and went downstairs to the guest room for the night. Marilyn remained in the master bedroom upstairs. There were no showers because the water wasn't working. We did have the water we had brought to drink, and our trusty cell phones still had some minutes available.

The next morning, we called Art and Chuck. They offered to drive north to rescue us, but we turned down their offer until we knew that main roads in this private area were drivable. We explained that we were separated from society and would have to take a boat to leave the area because of the fallen trees. Help was sure to come eventually.

In the morning we ate on the deck in the sunshine and continued working on our book. We decided that under the circumstances, it was best to be with a longtime friend. We talked, shared, laughed, and worked on the manuscript. Afterward, we raked and gathered piles of rubble on the side lot lines.

Our neighbors boated over and took our cell phones into town to be charged. They had communicated with some friends who lived on the main road who had electricity, and they could check what was happening outside of our isolated area.

Upon their return, they reported that the main road was open and power company workers had used chain saws to enter our private road. They inspected downed poles and lines. With help from other Michigan power companies, the workers thought they could return by the end of the week to make replacements and repairs.

Late Monday afternoon, friends from the area used chain saws to clear a two-track exit from our driveways to the main road. By Tuesday afternoon, we were able to leave the area and head home to Grand Rapids. Although life had been primitive for two days, we were thankful to be alive and were excited to reunite with our families.

Much work had to be done on the grounds after the insurance inspectors checked the area.

The work would be completed at a later date.

This private Lake Leelanau area was one of the worst hit by the windstorm. The path of destruction ran from Glen Arbor to Mission Peninsula in this particular northern Michigan region.

When Marilyn and I discussed having an adventure, never could we have imagined experiencing a straight-line windstorm. However, we shall never forget the August 2015 summer experience, but it didn't stop us from seeking more adventures.

Godfrey-Lee Book Dedication

"Hey, Thelm, are you ready for another adventure?" I asked Carol. "Sure," she answered. "What do you have in mind, Lou?"

I explained that it was a secret, but to be ready at 10:00 a.m. the following morning and I would pick her up.

Carol was ready to go when I arrived, and we headed toward the southwest side of Grand Rapids. She asked where we were heading as I pulled off the expressway onto Burton Avenue.

I told her that we had an appointment at the district office of the Godfrey-Lee Public Schools.

We would present the office with two of *The Promised Piece* books, a paperback and a hardback copy, and then we

Lee School district office book dedication

would visit our old LHS neighborhood. It was my intent to explore many of the old places Carol and I frequented over fifty years ago.

"Wow! This will be a fun adventure," Carol said with a smile.

We got out of the car to meet the people in the district office. After talking about the publication of our book to the staff, we answered questions about how Lee School operated years ago during Carol's and my K-12 tenure.

Upon leaving, we decided to take a quick drive past the old Lee K-12 School Building. As we approached, the building basically looked the same as when we were students. We pulled over to the side of the avenue to share our impressions.

Memories surfaced as we remembered the location of the ice-skating rink behind the school in the winter months. We recalled the fun times we had skating after school in our elementary and middle school years.

I drove past many of our friends' old homes as we toured the community. Then I drove to Berkley and Delwood Avenues where Carol and I had resided during our younger years. We pulled in front of each of our old homes and reminisced about our growing-up years.

The houses looked much the same; however, the front yards seemed extra small, and the detached garages appeared further back on the lots than we had recalled.

When we drove by my old home, we noticed that the huge front porch was no longer a part of the old Lutke family house, and the front entranceway had changed. When we reached the Ford's home, we recalled the fun parties held at Carol's residence in the past.

"Remember the vacant lot across from my house?" Carol asked.

It was a car lot now, and it seemed hard to believe that we used to ride our bikes on the trail.

We even climbed the billboards on this same spot. Those certainly were the good old days.

We remembered that somebody tattled on us, and we were forbidden by our parents to climb the billboards ever again. Of course, we never did. Instead, we put on musical shows in the Ford's double-stall garage. Friends, neighbor kids, and my sisters would come to see our rendition of movies and musicals we had seen. We would sing and dance, and we thought we were talented actresses.

In essence, our audience enjoyed the music we played on the portable record player (small 45 rpm records with plastic discs in the center and 72 rpm larger record albums). The audience, in actuality, enjoyed the cookies and treats we offered and not so much the extravaganza shows we presented.

Next Carol and I drove a block over to where we caught the city bus to travel to downtown Grand Rapids. We concluded that the bus stop must have moved, so we drove to the old gravel pit where, lo and behold, Battjes Park had been built on the grounds where the old gravel pit used to be located.

We pulled into the parking lot and thought we would explore the park, until it started to rain.

Carol and I talked for a while in the car, and then decided to return at another time.

Our continuing excursion took us down Chicago Drive to find the Dairy Bar where we had purchased our ice cream treats and the old Jeanette's Grocery Store which had good nickel and dime candy in the day. All these establishments were gone as well as the Fry House. This was where the guys often hung out after dropping their dates off at their homes.

We continued driving down Chicago Drive and noticed that the old funeral home, hardware store, and Soda Bar were no longer in operation. Only one former grocery store still remained at the same location.

As we traveled down memory lane, we passed the Catholic church and attached school on the way to the Lee athletic fields on Godfrey Avenue. We drove around the area, passed more homes that we could still identify, and we ended up on Burton Street where the old Galewood Show had stood along with a grocery store and a corner bar.

Now a Dollar Store replaced some of the old establishments, but one furniture store and a drug store remained where we remembered them when we were growing up.

"What a fun adventure we had today," Carol said as we drove to Burton Heights and located the photography studio where we had our senior pictures taken many years ago.

On the way to South Division Avenue, we found where the pizza parlor, the foot-long hot dog drive-in restaurant, and other places we had enjoyed as teens had been located. We also found the Brann's Restaurant where our class would meet for a luncheon in another month.

We stopped for a Mexican lunch at the Beltline Bar and enjoyed the good food from yesteryear. Over margaritas we talked about the day and decided we would return for another adventure when we could explore Battjes Park. Perhaps, we would have a future park bench conversation there.

Our Third Adventure

The following summer our adventure included a trip back to our old stomping grounds. This time we went to the Godfrey-Lee district office again to pick up the picture depicting Carol and me presenting our book to the school last year.

We also stopped to see the damage which occurred at Lee School just months prior. The roof caved in on one side of the building, and there was construction taking place. We looked but didn't get out of the car. We hoped that repairs would be completed before school started in the fall.

Wonderful memories came to mind of the fabulous fifties and of 1960 when we graduated from high school.

One year before, we had explored the neighborhoods around the school, and this time we counted the five churches which surround the area. Only one had changed its name over the years.

After driving to Battjes Park, Carol and I walked around the compound and checked out the water hole where someone was fishing. We walked around the basketball courts and the baseball diamond and found only picnic tables. There were no park benches available for us to sit and discuss our day.

We decided to drive through Pinery Park, which was another local park in the Lee School vicinity. That would lead us to Twenty-Eighth Street where, in our younger years, many of our past afternoon and evening activities had taken place.

Fun times at the Beltline Drive-In Theater

We drove through the familiar park as we continued to Rogers Shopping Plaza, which is still in operation. Upon slowly inspecting the plaza, we ventured past the location of the old Beltline Drive-In Theater. We recalled dollar night, when we would pack kids into the car and go to a movie at the drive-in.

Cruising around Wyoming, Carol and I found the old Rogers Department Store building which was no longer in operation. It had been one of our favorite shopping spots for years, and the store gave S & H Green Stamps which was a bonus at that time.

While driving down Twenty-Eighth Street, Carol and I came to the conclusion that this area had changed considerably since we had last shopped in Wyoming. Some of the restaurants and banks still remained, but other than Roger's Plaza, hardly any of the stores we frequented in the earlier years were still in operation.

> The fun adventures we enjoyed together in the past and the memories that remain, continued to give us joy as we smiled and chatted about our remembrances of long ago.

The fun adventures we enjoyed together in the past and the memories that remain, continued to give us joy as we smiled and chatted about our remembrances of long ago.

On our way home, we decided that all in all, it had been a good return adventure. Thelm and Lou explored some additional territory in the old neighborhood, and this adventure left us with many happy thoughts about our younger years as students at Lee School.

Marketing Our Book

Speaking of adventures, we discussed the possibility of marketing our book with someone local to advise us. This certainly would be a different type of adventure for Carol and me.

The introduction to Diane, our literary agent, occurred after Carol and I had met an acquaintance of mine, Susan, at a church function that summer. Carol attended the function with me, and Susan happened to inquire if Carol and I were longtime friends. She knew not that we had a lifetime friendship history since kindergarten.

After we mentioned our recently published book, Susan liked what she heard and suggested that we might want to meet Diane Jones, a local friend of hers, who could guide us. If we were interested, we could make an appointment with Diane about marketing our book. (God works in mysterious ways.)

Carol and I gave Susan a copy of *The Promised Piece* and discussed the possibility of meeting with Diane after she and Susan read our friendship story. When that happened, there were some suggestions that the two women had shared about extending our story.

Meeting Our Literary Agent

We had an introductory meeting with Diane, and she encouraged us to continue our journey by expanding our friendship story. She explained that *The Promised Piece* was too long for a short story and too short for a novel.

She added that our characters were established, and then suggested that by visiting more park benches, our friendship and our lives should continue to be shared with others. Our

story was a testimony of our faithfulness to God, to our longtime relationship, and with our greater friendship group of Draco sisters.

Before we made the decision to continue writing, Carol and I talked with Art and Chuck.

They requested a meeting with Diane to hear more about the plans for our extended book.

Diane Jones, our literary agent

We made a date with Diane to meet before Christmas. Art and Chuck attended the meeting with us, and after we listened to Diane's rationale, they asked a few questions. Then their blessings were given to Carol and me to go ahead with our second book. It was important for us to have their moral support for this project. We wanted our soulmates to understand the obligation we had made.

The Completion of Past Experiences

When Carol and I read Part I, the backstory of our journey, the chapters concluded with most of our past adventures. We knew we must let go of yesterday and concentrate on our present days as we travel forward with our second book. However, we also realized that memories would resurface throughout the entire book.

We felt blessed and thankful that we still are going strong. Our hearts are huge when it comes to loving our Father in heaven, our families, and our group of friends. We look ahead to many more years of joy on our friendship journey.

At this point, Carol and I are in our seventies, and we still enjoy spending time together and having park bench conversations. Thelm and Lou decided to keep extending the adventures in both Florida and in Michigan for as long as possible.

We have taken trips together as couples to Europe, and we still travel with our husbands and with other groups. Hopefully, these trips will continue for as long as we are able to take journeys.

Up to this point, most of our travel plans had happened as planned. We never thought about having to cancel a trip due to bad health or for reasons beyond our control. When this did happen, we were shocked.

Along Life's Pathway

God has been good to us. He has granted Carol the ability to survive a serious stroke and has sustained her through some trying times. He has also given both of us a second chance at marriage, travel opportunities, and has enabled us to write a second story together in our senior years.

Our lives are filled with positive experiences as we carry on serving the Lord and living each day in the present. By having faith and trust in God, we follow His promise to fear not as He guides us along the pathway of life.

PART II

park bench
conversations
(the present)

our gift

CHAPTER SEVENTEEN

bring on the park benches

Reeds Lake

Carol and I felt uplifted as we started a whole new chapter of our lives. The idea of starting afresh beckoned us to Collins Park in East Grand Rapids. It was the perfect time for a park bench conversation.

We have always felt comfortable at this park because we both lived in the southeast suburbs of Grand Rapids while raising our children. Now in our retirement, we both live close to that area once again. This familiar location makes it easier to meet for luncheon dates, have park bench conversations, get ice cream treats, and plan our next Thelm and Lou adventure.

Sitting on the park bench today, we looked out over Reeds Lake and reminisced about Ramona Amusement Park of yesteryear. It had stood on this property from 1897 to 1955.

The delicious caramel corn was Carol's favorite remembrance, while I recalled the steamship that took people around the lake as our families ate dinner on the huge deck. After we ate, the real fun began with the rides and all the

Jersey Junction enjoying ice cream

sounds and smells of Ramona Amusement Park, which were now coming back to life in our minds.

We could almost hear the melodic circus-like music as we continued talking about this beloved park which was packed full of childhood memories.

Our fond memory included the rides—the merry-go-round, the pony rides, and especially the breathtaking derby racer ride. As we continued to converse about the wonderful times we had cherished as youngsters, we realized why we still are making visits to this park in our adulthood.

Truly it was usually older relatives—our aunts and uncles, or even our parents—who experienced the skating rink and the theater in the park. That was where big-name entertainers came to perform many years before our time.

There was a feeling of déjà vu, almost an uncanny feeling that we had skated or been present at a performance at the theater as guests. Of course, Carol and I understood that we had not been present because we were far too young at that time.

Today, we felt a part of the former setting as it appeared yesterday, and we understood why we still enjoy Collins Park today. It is a special feeling to spend relaxing hours in this park-bench setting with a longtime friend.

> We have encountered a new stage of our lives, and we must make the most of each moment.

What we specifically remember are the visits to the Reeds Lake area as teenagers, attending high school games at East Grand Rapids High School, boating on Reeds Lake, and walking the route around the lake. Add to that the shopping and dining at Gaslight Village on Wealthy Street. How can we forget our ice cream stops at Jersey Junction?

I personally pictured my mother, who had attended Sunday school at the Lake Drive Church as a child. That's where my parents were married and brought up their five children.

Mother adored her small church, and her funeral was held there, just blocks from the park.

A condominium now sits on that corner in East Grand Rapids. However, the special people who attended the church are left with loving spiritual memories which they shall forever hold in their hearts.

Presently, Carol and I are comfortable at Collins Park, eating at Rose's Restaurant, having park bench conversations, and just strolling around the lake. One more important stop at the end of our visits is to enjoy a tasty ice cream dessert at Jersey Junction.

Retirees

Carol and I talked about a certain amount of leisure time which we have experienced as retirees. We have time to reflect on things we like to do in the present, which brings us pleasure in our day-to-day lives. It is then that we realize, we have encountered a new stage of our lives, and we must make the most of each moment.

We are more available for family outings, to pursue favorite hobbies, and for various travel plans. It is also important for us to do daily devotions with our husbands and to attend non-work-related meetings and luncheons during the day. In the past, there had seldom been enough time to consistently do these things.

After raising our families and being employed for years, Carol and I found it refreshing to do things at a slower pace. We agreed that we have more opportunities to make choices during the retirement years of our lives.

Upon retirement, Carol and I did not particularly feel as though we had aged or would ever model our mothers or grandmothers before us. We still felt young at heart and appreciated a new sense of freedom. We continued to be free to make decisions about our future years without having certain restraints that held us back. Now, we focused on enjoyment according to God's will for our lives.

However, overnight it seemed to happen. Our bodies weren't quite as flexible as they had been in the past. We also seemed to get tired more easily. Friends our age are now taking naps, going to bed sooner at night, and rising much earlier in the morning.

Carol and I decided we would go to bed later at night and sleep later in the morning. Afterall, isn't that what true retirement is all about? We thought it was. Our new theme seems to promote relaxation more and to let things happen naturally.

Reinventing Ourselves

Carol's routine includes walking and doing water aerobics to physically stay in shape. Her favorite things to do in retirement are to attend womens meetings, play Mahjong, watch old movies, and view Michigan State University football and basketball games with Chuck.

Art and I walk almost every day; if not in our neighborhood, we hike at parks or nature trails, and go to the beach or wherever we can explore God's beauteous nature.

The waterskiing I used to love to do went along the wayside in my seventies. I jumped into the lake at our cottage and told my son, the captain of the boat, that I was going skiing. My grandkids looked at me and knew their Grammy would try to do this. Unfortunately, my arms would not support me for more than a few minutes.

> Carol and I aren't the physically active schoolgirls we used to be, but we both remain positive as we realize how important it is to stay healthy, active, and happy.

157

For now, the skiing, skating, golf, and tennis are not on the top of my priority list. I shall continue doing my aerobic exercises, lifting small weights, biking, walking, reading, writing, and doing puzzles of any kind. All these things help to keep my body and mind active. Because Art is a March Madness fan, I am a total college basketball nut for several weeks each spring.

Carol and I aren't the physically active schoolgirls we used to be, but we both remain positive as we realize how important it is to stay healthy, active, and happy.

Our church lives are important to us, and we have both taken leadership roles as we participate in various groups, volunteer, and stay active socially. Carol serves on the Missions Committee, and I will be a greeter, now that my two-year term as president of the Women's Fellowship ended this spring. Both Carol and I attend Bible study classes and luncheon groups, in addition to other special events offered at the United Church of Marco Island, in Florida.

Discussions, and Then What?

Sitting on a park bench stimulates Carol's and my minds, as we move forward in our ongoing friendship journey of writing our extended book. It also gives us a perfect excuse to see each other, and to engage in fun and interesting times together.

Of course, never forget the reward at the end of our serious discussions—the ice cream parlors in both Michigan and Florida which bring us so much joy. Whenever Carol and I need communication, we decide it is time for a park bench conversation, and we know that at the end of a comfortable park bench conversation, without a doubt, we enjoy an ice cream treat.

We try not to concentrate on things that can't be accomplished, instead we keep busy and happy doing things that we can complete. We are thankful to be alive and active. Our plan is to do our best possible with the abilities which we still have.

CHAPTER EIGHTEEN

senior moments

Draco Sister Time

When meeting with the Draco sisters in the summer, Carol and I spoke about the extension of the book, and I explained that we would like to add a bit of reality and humor to the middle part of our journey. I explained that because of our age, we are more apt to have "senior moments." Perhaps we could share a few of these events with our "bestie friends."

That is exactly what the Draco sisters did as we sat at a table having lunch and enjoying each other's company.

Laughter filled the room as each sister shared a humorous or even embarrassing moment. We can laugh at ourselves and at each other because we are all in the senior-moment stage of life together.

When the ladies asked me for an example of my personal senior moment that I would submit for the book, this is how I led the way.

Marilyn: One day as I dressed, I put on a black outfit, complete with black shoes. My job was to present at the Kent Intermediate School District (KISD) to a group of educators in

Kent County. I had retired, but still occasionally presented at in-service programs.

When I arrived at the KISD parking lot, I looked down at my feet and discovered that I had two different colored shoes on. Staring back up at me were a black shoe and a navy-blue shoe, the same style, just different colors.

I jumped back into the car, drove home to correct the situation, and then rushed back to give my presentation.

I shared with my audience what I had done, calling it a "senior moment." The teachers laughed and shared their senior moments. All this happened before the actual in-service began. It warmed up the audience, and an excellent dinner followed an energetic in-service meeting.

On the way home that evening, I realized that I could have pulled this shoe incident off even if someone had noticed my mismatched shoes. However, it was my decision to change my navy shoe, and to put another pair of black shoes in my trunk. One never knows when a senior "oops" moment will happen again!

Carol: Laughingly, she explained that ever since being a teenager, she liked to drive and was proud of her driving ability. She still likes to drive.

However, there is one exception which she will never forget. Her senior moment happened when she dropped Chuck off at a men's luncheon at a restaurant in downtown Grand Rapids. Concentrating on the people walking into the restaurant, she failed to notice until too late that there was a curb right there. In fact, when she drove over the curb in front of the restaurant, her face turned a bright red from embarrassment. Especially because Chuck's friends saw her do it.

Chuck looked at Carol and asked, "Drive much?"

As Carol proceeded to drive off the curb, she thought about the teenager who was invincible years ago.

Judy: Judy humbly asked me to use the following conversation for her senior moment in the book.

Valentine's Day is Judy's birthday, and I called to wish her both a happy birthday and a happy Valentine's Day on her special day.

After asking Judy how she was celebrating her birthday, she told me that she was going to lunch with her daughter. She asked what I was doing that day.

I mentioned that I was attending a Valentine's Day luncheon and style show with some friends at the yacht club in a few hours.

Judy remarked that she didn't know that Cascade had a yacht club.

After pausing for a minute, I reminded Judy that I was calling her from Florida and that I was going to the Marco Island Yacht Club for the afternoon.

We giggled for a few minutes, and then Judy admitted that she had forgotten that I wasn't in Michigan, and that I was calling her from Florida instead.

Donna: Our sister Donna sent me several senior moments—some funny incidents which are common occurrences for seniors. The first one is when she didn't think it was necessary to make a grocery list. She said that she knew exactly what ingredients she needed at the grocery store. After all she could remember four items. However, she scribbled the items down on a piece of paper anyway. When she arrived at the store, she could only recall two items. The other two would not come to her mind. So, she pulled out her list only to discover that she couldn't read her own scribbles.

Donna walked up and down the aisles trying to find clues to remind her of the ingredients she needed for her recipe. Eventually she walked down the correct aisle and located the items, wondering why this short trip took her so long to complete.

Donna's next incident was when she backed out of the driveway at her home, and then remembered that she needed a particular item from inside of the house.

She pulled back into the driveway, got out of the car, and hurried to retrieve the item she had forgotten. However, when she returned to get back into her car, there was no vehicle.

The car had rolled down the driveway and stopped across the street in a vacant lot. She had forgotten to put the vehicle into parking gear.

Donna will never forget how she felt when her car was missing. When she found it, she had only herself to blame.

Donna said, "Thank goodness, the car was in one piece with no scrapes, but mainly it didn't hit anyone or anything!"

Her final senior moment is far too cute to omit.

Donna was in church with her husband, Arn, where a little boy sitting in the pew in front of them was misbehaving. As the child's father carried the child out of the sanctuary, the child dramatically shouted, "Pray for me!"

According to Donna, the occurrence brought some smiles, mainly because as grandparents, many of us can relate to the little tyke, and yet find humor in the situation.

Sharon: Sharon and her husband, Mel, have only one grand-daughter named Sian. As they were visiting with Sian, the topic of weddings came up.

Mel asked Sian if she thought she would have a big wedding someday. Actually, pretty grownup stuff for Sian at the tender age of seven.

They expected a sweet little girl answer. However, much to her grandparents' chagrin, Sian retorted (without any malice or forethought), "Maybe Papa and you won't be there for my wedding, cuz you're old and you could be dead by then."

Talk about a reality check!

Jackie: After hearing noises in her laundry room in the lower level of their home, and not realizing where the sound was coming from, Jackie forgot about it.

A few days later she smelled something odd in her laundry room, so she decided to explore. It was then that Jackie opened the dryer door and found a dead rat had gotten into the vent and had died inside the dryer.

Horrified, she called her husband, Harv, to remove the ugly rodent. She wondered why she hadn't thought to check the dryer vent earlier.

One More Senior Moment

For a summertime luncheon, the girls met at a restaurant a distance away. Carol and I, who always are on time, were late that day.

The girls called us and wondered where we were and inquired if everything was alright, since we usually arrive early.

We told them to go ahead and order, and that we would join them for dessert.

Actually, Carol and I had a senior moment together and we are sharing it now. Carol had picked me up, and we decided to take M-6, which would give us more than enough time to meet our sisters at the restaurant.

Wrong! I decided to interview Carol regarding their wedding anniversary which took place a week prior. As I continued asking questions and recording answers, Carol continued driving, and neither of us paid any attention to the exits.

Finally, Carol asked if we had gone too far, as we were approaching Zeeland. We had gone several miles beyond our exit, so we got off from the expressway. By the time we found the restaurant, we arrived in time for dessert.

The ladies didn't question us too much because one of the other gals was late as well, and another sister admitted she had trouble finding the restaurant.

Carol and I laughed because I had picked a bouquet of flowers for sister, Donna. We brought the flowers inside the restaurant for a centerpiece.

I told the sisters, we stopped to pick the flowers in a field, and that was the reason why we were late. Carol and I knew full-well that was an excuse for getting lost in our book interview, and the girls also knew I was kidding them.

Our Gift: A few laughs, a few tears, friends are blessings through the years.

Forever Friendship Piece

Forever Friendships – Carol (Ford) Jennings

As the years passed, the Draco girls got married, had children, and eventually became grandparents. A few members of the group are now great-grandparents. Over the years, the girls would see each other occasionally for important events. These were extremely busy years, but with only a telephone call, we were ready to get together again.

Today our conversations turn to aging. The women are interested in the health problems each of our family members are experiencing. Then one member will say, "Remember when this happened at Lee High School?" The laughter rings throughout the room and the girls are sixteen again.

The nine women rally around one another. We lived through divorce, widowhood, and the loss of children and parents. We are strong, we are invincible, and we will be together until the end. Then the laughter will be heard throughout the halls of heaven.

Carol miraculously survived a debilitating stroke, and she makes my heart sing. She is an inspiration to the Draco sisters and to our classmates, because she represents love, hope, and a positive attitude toward life. The Draco group is happy to have our friend, so vital after many difficult years of rehabilitation and healing. We pray for many more years of good health for Carol and Chuck.

CHAPTER NINETEEN

a favorite florida setting

Leigh Plummer Park

About a year after Carol's stroke, we selected Leigh Plummer Park in Florida as our first ever place to have a park bench conversation. She picked the park which was close to her church, and it now was also Art's and my church. This park, along with our favorite bench, held a significant meaning for both of us.

The past several years indicated a more normal time in Florida and Michigan during our early retirement years. Our topics included enjoyable visits with our Draco school friends, family time, an overview of some travels, and a pending class reunion.

Our Gift: The opportunity to sit on park benches enjoying God's creation with a friend is valuable, well-spent time.

In the Present

This day was a clear warm day, and we were happy to be together as we enjoyed the gentle breeze and various flowering bushes. It was not difficult to delight in the scenery, as birds gracefully flew around the pond, and people walked around Plummer Park. One woman was doing yoga in the distance, and a child was riding a bicycle.

Carol and I remembered a park bench conversation shortly after her stroke. At that time, she was slowly learning how to speak again.

I said the word, "God," followed by, "Did God have a role in your survival?"

Carol remarked, "Center!"

I asked if she meant that God was the center of everything. She nodded her head, squeezed my hand, and replied, "Yes!"

Carol shared that God wasn't ready to take her home after the stroke. He assured her that there was still work to be done on this earth. She feels He granted her a longer life to fulfill that work.

Today, Carol can speak in complete sentences. Looking out over the pond, I thought of the improvements she had physically and cognitively made. We very much understood that, indeed, God is the center of the universe. He holds the universe in the palm of His hands.

Our Gift: Giving thanks to almighty God for all His gifts.

Relatives Visit

Carol told me about Chuck's cousins who were coming to visit them on the Isles of Capri the following week. In fact, Chuck's sister, Jill, and her husband were staying with them at their condominium for this small reunion. The cousins had rented a house in the area. Many outings were planned.

Art and I were expecting our children and our grandchildren to visit. Carol and I looked forward to seeing our families over the winter months and spring break.

It was delightful to be back in Florida with the familiarity of the area and the palm trees, but mostly the warmth of the beautiful sunshine as two forever friends sat on our favorite park bench enjoying life.

Projecting Ahead

Carol and I continued to brainstorm about which parks we wanted to visit this season. We knew we would visit both Hammock Bay and the Isles of Capri. We added the Esplanade Marina and Mackle Park to our list. Then we took the elevator upstairs in the tower to read from the manuscript on my laptop computer in Art's and my condo.

We discussed the transition of moving from the past into the present time of our lives. Part II of our journey had started, and it was with much expectation that we planned to live our lives by asking God to lead the way.

Wherever we go, Carol and I feel ultra-comfortable sitting on a park bench in a quiet area. Some benches are stationary, some swing, some are fancy, and some are plain, ordinary, hard benches. However, they usually have a nice view if located in a park.

We had spent so much time on benches, but our favorite one allowed us to swing as we talked. Many conversations had taken place at precise spots. Oh, if these benches had ears, the stories they could tell.

Transition Time

Today, Carol looked me square in the eyes and said, "Marilyn, I have had a difficult time transitioning after our sudden move to Cook Valley Estates at the end of 2017. Because things happened ultrafast, I felt like I had been in a whirl-wind."

For several years Carol and Chuck had lived in the lake-shore area near Lake Michigan. Their first condo in Grand Haven overlooked the channel leading to the Big Lake. Then, after moving to a home on Spring Lake, Carol and Chuck's final purchase was a condo on the Grand River, all near the beaches and marinas.

"Now, we are in the city again, and I can't get my head around this last move to Grand Rapids and all the changes," Carol shared.

The fact was that Chuck had a second diagnosis of cancer and needed radiation treatments in Grand Rapids at a cancer center. That was the reason for their move.

They had made the decision to list their Spring Lake con-do and made the move to Cook Valley Estates, an Indepen-dent Senior Retirement Home.

Due to the change happening so quickly, Carol was try-ing to make sense of everything that had transpired the last several weeks and months.

We talked about the transitions which Carol thought she would have to make now that they had moved into a Cook Valley apartment. In the summer and fall months, they will reside in the "big house," which is a senior living indepen-dent unit.

She continued to pray about it and hoped to get involved with the women living there. Perhaps, she will join a book club, swim in the indoor pool, play Mahjong, and even join a Michigan P.E.O. upon her return to Grand Rapids.

Carol remained open to various options. I knew she would eventually transition well once she felt organized. That meant getting familiar with the area stores, malls, churches, and restaurants in the greater Grand Rapids area again.

Our Sisters

As the wind picked up, we continued talking about our Draco sisters and the fact that they liked our first book. They were surprised that we were expanding the book when we mentioned it at our last Christmas luncheon in December.

Carol and I suspected that the women would feel differently in the future when we shared some of our proposed ideas with them. We talked about adding both fun topics and further personal discussion topics, which we would address in the middle chapters.

Health Issues

The topic of health problems which were occurring in our group surfaced and the importance of considering these serious health issues as we continued our journey.

It is a fact that as we age, there will be more decisions to make in our twilight years. There may be trials concerning our health, probable injuries, and possibly additional moves to senior villages and even care homes for our Draco sisters and their husbands.

No matter what happens, Carol and I know that we will be sensitive to the changes which occur as we reflect about natural transitions at this stage of our lives.

Finally, we went to the car. It was time for ice cream at Sweet Annie's. These two friends needed a break and a treat, so we sat outdoors and continued talking and enjoyed the moment over ice cream.

Our Gift: To pray for God's protection for the sick and hurting, as they age.

The Coming Months

It seems ironic that we usually started our conversations in January at Hammock Bay, where Art and I lived, and we often completed our conversation on the Isles of Capri, where the Jennings reside.

After an interesting afternoon of casual talking, I dropped Carol off near her condominium development. We waved and knew we would see the Jennings on Sunday at church, before Art and I left for Michigan.

"Later gator" could be heard as Carol walked up the path to her condominium.

Farewell

After church the final Sunday, we stopped at Leigh Plummer Park with our husbands. We walked directly to the familiar park bench which Carol and I still call our own.

We bid our park a final good-bye and felt that we would be back again the following year. I whispered a silent prayer of thanksgiving for all the time we spent together on this bench. It had been our first park bench and so many conversations had started at this locale. It felt like we were saying farewell to a familiar object that we hated to leave.

CHAPTER TWENTY

michigan summer celebrations

Beautiful Park Visits

After the Jennings arrived in Michigan for the summer months, Carol and I decided that we would first visit Collins Park, which is located close to our homes.

We sat on a bench and jotted down a summer/fall schedule which included meeting with Diane, our literary agent, to go over our progress and get input from her regarding the rough draft of the manuscript.

In June, the class of 1960 would hold a reunion planning meeting, and there would be luncheons and visits with our friendship group. Carol and I looked forward to fun summer and fall months of activities with our forever friends.

June Outings

The ladies met at a restaurant, and after eating we proceeded to talk about health issues which were happening both in our group and with our husbands. After a short discussion, we forged ahead with many exciting plans for the year.

Upon meeting at Marty's home, the committee set a date for the reunion and decided on the location. After lunch and socialization, we left with our specific duties. Once the date was verified with the club, the email was sent to classmates to mark their calendars for the upcoming class reunion.

Cook Valley Communication

Upon arriving at Cook Valley Estates, where Carol and Chuck reside, I parked the car. Carol and I walked to the gazebo area. There were tables which overlooked a medium-sized pond on the lush grounds. We relaxed and enjoyed the late summer afternoon, including the lovely outdoor landscape.

We continued our conversation which included the reunion planning meeting. It had been exciting seeing the committee members as we planned our 60/60 Reunion. Next fall, the class of 1960 would be celebrating their sixtieth year since graduation from high school, minus one-third of the class who had passed away.

We looked at each other and could hardly believe that time had gone by so quickly. We still remembered our high school graduation and how we appeared in our 1960 Echo Yearbook pictures.

About that time, a swarm of bugs darted at Carol and me, so we decided to move indoors to protect ourselves, and to gaze at the lovely gazebo area from a window above. But other people were sitting in this room, so Carol walked me to my car. We waved, and I headed home after a busy and memorable day.

Ada Park

Carol and I stopped for a lunch on the porch at a restaurant in Ada. As we ate, our conversation included Art's and my Greek Isles and Italian cruises which we had taken in May. Some of the highpoints were stopping in Montenegro, Crete, Mykonos, Athens, Santorini, and the Amalfi Coast.

The Jennings were looking forward to various family summer outings in Michigan, then a Caribbean Cruise in the fall.

We sat on an Ada Park bench and talked for a while, and then walked to a shaded picnic table area where we spread out the manuscript. When it got windy, we picked up our manuscript and headed to the local ice cream shop where we continued our conversation over our favorite dessert.

Before Carol and I left, we decided to introduce some additional discussion topics to the Draco women this season.

A Gift: To enjoy each new day which is given to us by our Father, because He loves and protects us.

Beautiful Tassel Park 2019

Carol and I had our next park bench conversation at Tassel Park on a beautiful summer afternoon. The bench we selected overlooked the Thornapple River in Cascade Township, and we could see the dam and hear the water splashing from a distance.

We read from the manuscript and made a few decisions about what our Florida expectations would be for the winter months. Somehow, family concerns and future outings became the subject of our conversation. Then, can you believe that our car automatically headed toward the ice cream shop, indicating we needed to purchase a cool refreshing dish of ice cream?

Emery/Ripperda Family Reunion

Carol asked about our family reunion which had been celebrated on Mackinac Island in early June and wondered if I had some pictures of the event.

I explained that twenty-nine family members met at Mackinaw City. We took the ferry boat to the Mission Point Lodge for our stay on the island.

Our children had come from four different states to be with the family, and my niece, Vicki, made a surprise appearance from Colorado. Therefore, we had a total of thirty relatives together, celebrating three days of fun and frolic.

As a group, we walked to the lodge where we registered and awaited our luggage delivered by horse-drawn taxis. There are no cars on the island, so people either walk, bike, or take horse drawn carriages to their destinations.

The family was free to unpack or explore the island, but it was requested that they return by six o'clock to meet in our private family dining room overlooking the Straits of Mackinac.

Before dinner, I welcomed our family and reminded them about the saying, "The family that *prays* together *stays* together." This was a phrase that their deceased Grandfather Lutke had repeated in the past.

Next, Art spoke and led the family in a prayer before dinner. At "Amen," Vicki seemed to have magically appeared and surprised her cousins. After welcome hugs, we quieted down and were served a delicious family dinner.

Emery/Ripperda Family Reunion

We thought the grandchildren would want to go play miniature golf, swim in the pool, or further explore the area around the lodge. Instead, everyone stayed in the private dining room as we socialized well into the evening. Others went on the outdoor balcony overlooking the lush grounds and the Straits of Mackinac. Everyone stayed well into the evening.

Breakfast was served the next morning in the same dining area. Then the family members were excused to go hike, bike ride, golf, swim, shop, or purchase freshly made fudge. They could also explore the beaches, trails, Fort Mackinac, Arch Rock, the Butterfly House, museums, churches, island eateries, and the famous Grand Hotel.

All in all, it was an awesome reunion, and it was sad to bid everyone good-bye as we returned by ferry to head home.

Brenda and Dean's family took the ferry boat to Saint Ignace in the Upper Peninsula of Michigan, which is located north of the Mackinac Bridge. They went for an extended vacation. The rest of the family went to Mackinaw City where their cars were parked. Some families went immediately home, while others headed to the family summer home on Lake Leelanau for additional time together.

Many pictures and memories of the family reunion of 2019 were taken to forever remind us of a sweet moment in time.

Meeting with Diane

Upon arriving back to Grand Rapids, Carol and I met with Diane, our literary agent. The purpose of the meeting was to go over the manuscript which explained how much had been accomplished up to this point on our story.

We alluded to the special relationship that the three of us have, and we spoke about the direction that the final section of our book was taking.

For the conclusion of the story, we discussed the idea of meditations written by the Draco sisters. We explained that with a focus on the future, individual meditations would give purpose to our inspirational story.

Carol and I had requested that our Draco sisters would please contribute pieces over the next several months. We did not put any pressure on them to do so. It would be a choice for each woman to write an article from their heart.

As Carol and I strolled to the car after the meeting, we decided that the local ice cream shop, which was just a block away, was calling for us to pay a visit.

Our Gift: God brings particular people into our lives for a purpose.

Visit to Holland

Each August the Draco sisters visit Sandy in Holland near her birthday. We bring her cards and hugs, with the hope that she still recognizes us.

Dementia is a disease which takes memory away. However, we love to see Sandy's smiles. We hope our actions and voices make her feel loved and comfortable. It makes her sisters happy to spend time with her.

Susan, Sandy's daughter, takes pictures of the group. She is always available when we come to visit her mother in the memory unit fireplace room.

After our visit, the sisters leave and go to lunch. We enjoy an afternoon of dining, reminiscing, and planning future luncheons. This particular day, we also discussed the progression of the book, and we reminded our sisters to submit their meditational pieces for the final chapters of the second book. They asked a few questions and seemed to understand that the conclusion of the book would be worked on after the class reunion in 2020.

On the way home, Carol and I talked about our visit today, and how difficult it was to see Sandy's condition decline. It was disheartening to view the changes in a person who used to be so vibrant.

However, the Draco sisters will visit Sandy each year for as many years as possible. We pray for God's blessings on her and her family.

Chuck's Big Birthday

Chuck and his younger sister, Jill, share a birthday on the same day. Jill was turning seventy and Chuck would be eighty in September. Their children had planned a birthday party for them at the Spring Lake Country Club.

The families arrived from five different states at David's beach home on the shores of Lake Michigan on a Friday afternoon. They had dinner at their son David's cottage the first night and then went to the Spring Lake Holiday Inn, where the family had rooms for the weekend.

They went back to the cottage on Saturday after brunch and spent the afternoon at the beach.

After showering and getting ready for the celebration, they drove to the country club in the evening. The family was prepared for the birthday bash.

Cocktails were served as their favorite rock 'n' roll music played in the background. The relatives shared tidbits of news while the guests enjoyed the music and socialized. They ate a lovely dinner outdoors overlooking the lush golf course, and then it was time to toast Jill and Chuck. Family members continued to tell little tales about the guests of honor.

Carol's birthday was also in September, so she was toasted as well. After the candles were blown out and the birthday cake was served, the special autumn birthdays were celebrated in a festive manner.

The family continued talking until they headed back to David's beach home in Grand Haven.

Later, the family stayed at the Spring Lake Holiday Inn for the second night.

After eating brunch in the morning at the inn, some family members headed home while others made one last stop back to the beach house for the afternoon. Everyone had a good time, and many memories were made that weekend.

Lunch and Ada Park

Carol picked me up and we went to lunch at our favorite eatery in Ada, where we sat on the porch enjoying the fall weather and the delicious food.

Next, we drove to Ada Park. After hiking down a trail to the pond and park bench area, we found a comfortable place to settle into.

We spoke of raising our children in the faith and prayed that they too would bring our grandchildren up in Christian-centered homes. My son has a wooden message on his fireplace that states, "As for me and my house, we will serve the Lord" (Josh. 24:15 KJV) Along with the words and actions, faith and Christian principles are important ingredients to pass from generation to generation.

Carol and I bid our Michigan park bench farewell. We knew the next time we would meet again, we would be at a sparkling Florida pond.

Past Trips

As Carol and I walked to our cars, we talked about trips that we both had recently taken. She told me about the trip they had enjoyed with close friends. They had cruised to Panama from Florida, taken a cruise through the Panama Canal, which ended in California. Then they flew back to Fort Lauderdale, Florida.

Art and I had taken a trip to northern Italy. We stayed on Lake Maggiore and Stressa, and other places included Siena, Florence, Verona, and the trip ended in Venice.

We looked forward to new travels this year. Art and I planned a May cruise to northern Italy with a travel group from the Florida Gulf Coast University. We also were taking a road trip in the British Isles, followed by a cruise to the Azores, Canary Islands, and Lisbon in the fall. This was our year for travel, as we would go to Las Vegas, Phoenix, and Tucson in November.

CHAPTER TWENTY-ONE

make a choice

Make a Choice

The Draco sisters met for a luncheon. After lunch, Carol was on a roll and added an interesting note to the conversation by asking a thought-provoking question. "If you could choose one person, living or dead, to sit on a park bench with for an hour, who would you choose to speak with? What questions would you ask that person?"

The girls sat quietly and thought for a few moments.

Judy answered first. She said her choice would be her only daughter, Lori. They would be relaxed as they discussed their family because there are fifty-four members, as of the last count. It is apparent that Lori and Judy would have much to discuss on that park bench.

Donna would want to speak with her mother, who is now deceased. She would ask questions about her maternal grandmother, because due to her early death, Donna never met her. Now that Donna is a great-grandmother herself, she would like to know more details about her grandmother to pass on to her children and grandchildren.

Sue said that she would choose someone involved with music. Her mother sang and played the piano and organ for church and for other people. She was very musically talented.

In school band, Sue played the clarinet and oboe, and she now wishes that she had continued using her music ability over the years. Therefore, she chose Jack McKindley, the deceased Lee School band director, to have a conversation about music on a park bench.

Jackie also chose her mother as the person to converse with. She said that there are many questions she would ask about her mother's past life. Jackie wishes that she knew more about her mother's family history to pass on to other family members.

Sharon chose President Abraham Lincoln. She has always been intrigued with Honest Abe.

She would inquire about his life as the president of the United States. Sharon wonders if the president ever wished he could have quit his job and have left the country for an easier life. His burden was extra heavy during the Civil War. It would be interesting to talk with him about his presidential years.

Carol recalls that she sometimes mouthed-off as a sixteen-year-old teenager. Sometimes her mother and she were like oil and water at that time. Carol wishes she could sit on a park bench to apologize to her mother for rebelling. Other than for that period, they had a wonderful relationship.

I, **Marilyn,** didn't have to think for very long. My father instantly came to mind. Dad was extra special to me. Due to serving in World War II, he was absent from my early life for several years. I will always remember the happiness as our family celebrated my father's return from the war. Dad and I were close. In fact, in his later life, we both were widowed at the same time, and we chose to spend time together during our grieving years. (Later we both remarried.)

As a Christian role model in our family, Dad was always available for his children, and I wish I would have asked him many more questions. Mainly questions about growing up, his school life, sports, jobs, and things of that nature.

Driving Home

On the way home from the luncheon, Carol and I discussed how we loved spending time caring and sharing with our Draco sisters. We noticed that most of the sisters chose family members to sit with on a park bench, one selected a teacher, and the other a past president.

It is amazing that after all these years, we are still learning things about each other, and that is a testimony to what friendship is all about. When we share our feelings, flaws, happy moments, even sad moments with each other, we continue to grow closer. Although our forever friendship group will become smaller over time, we plan to cherish every moment we can still spend together.

Additional Information

Upon further discussion, Carol and I decided to continue asking various people from different age groups the same question about a park bench choice. We would get a larger sample of answers.

Months later, we looked at the results, and concluded that most people chose to speak with a relative on a park bench, whether they were alive or deceased. Most would ask questions pertaining to family history or just sit and chat in an enjoyable area with a peaceful view.

Secondly, Jesus was chosen; and thirdly, a famous person was named. President Abraham Lincoln was often named. Others mentioned a favorite friend or a biblical character.

It was definitely an interesting question. We enjoyed hearing about the selection process and rationale of why people chose the person they preferred to sit with for a chat.

Our Gift: God gives us choices and expects us to make good decisions throughout life.

A Fun Remembrance

Carol directed a topic to our LHS sisters at another setting, and it was in regard to sharing their favorite birthday celebration. Our friends were asked to name which birthday it was and to tell when and why they chose it.

Donna said almost instantly that her sixteenth birthday luncheon came to mind. She had asked her mother to bake her favorite chicken loaf for her birthday luncheon. Donna requested this entree because it was so delicious. Surely the girls would love it as well.

Wrong! The Draco girls ate the rolls, veggie tray contents, fruit salad, birthday cake, and ice cream, but had cautiously picked at the famous chicken loaf.

Donna will never forget the look on our faces when the girls tasted the all-time famous dish.

To this day, Donna is still surprised that her friends didn't relish her delectable menu choice. (She still makes this dish for her family.)

Judy remembered the fiftieth surprise birthday party which had been given by their four children and their mates. It was a combined birthday party for their parents. They celebrate birthdays just a few weeks apart, and the gathering was a surprise for Judy and Rich.

She smiled as she recalled the fun her family had at the surprise party and how everyone had kept it a secret from them. The entire family attended the celebration. Judy and Rich will never forget that day.

Sharon's memory was of her birthday party in elementary school when she invited several of her school friends. For some reason Julie didn't attend the party. It seems that

Julie didn't make an appearance because the neighbor's huge Saint Bernard dog wouldn't let her pass the owner's house to arrive at Sharon's home. Julie was frightened of the large dog, so she turned around and went home with the present. Only later did Sharon learn why her classmate didn't attend the birthday party.

Sue shared that her favorite memory was when Mr. Warren took the Draco girls waterskiing at Kollen Park in Holland, Michigan. This picnic birthday party took place during our teenage years for Sue's July special day.

Sue's mother and her friend delivered the food, complete with a birthday cake for the celebration at the park. She recalls the fun the group had in the sunshine, eating a picnic lunch, skiing, and celebrating her summer birthday.

Carol remembers a special combined birthday/slumber party at her home. It was when the Draco girls celebrated four of the sister's birthdays together at one big birthday bash. Jackie, Carol, Sharon, and Marilyn had birthdays in the months of August through October, and they celebrated together. All the Draco girls attended the party, and it still remains Carol's favorite birthday memory of fun and frolic.

Marilyn – My tenth birthday party was a memorable childhood birthday memory. Five neighborhood friends, three girls and two boys, all lived on the same block, and we turned ten years old in the month of October. Our mothers planned a group celebration and invited *The Grand Rapids Press* to photograph the five of us enjoying birthday cake at one of the family homes.

We heard that one of the boys passed away as an adult, and the other attended a different school, so we lost contact with him when his family moved away. However, three of us graduated together from Lee High School.

It is endearing to recall favorite memories and to share them with your family and friends. It is indeed a gift to recall favorite times with special people, because your close family and friends can identify with your happiness.

Carol Hosted Her Sisters

Carol and I talked about the fall luncheon which the sisters recently held at a Cascade restaurant. After lunch, Carol had invited the group back to her Cook Valley apartment. After taking a tour through the big house and the Jennings apartment, the sisters spent the afternoon visiting before leaving for home.

Carol enjoyed having us come to see their place. The visit was pleasant, and the group planned our upcoming Christmas luncheon. It would take place at a restaurant in Grandville, followed with dessert at Sue's home in that area.

Many of the sisters and their husbands shared plans to travel to Florida for a month or more after the holidays. We understood that we would not see each other until the following year, but the sisters continued to communicate over the winter months.

Our Gift: Being together as friends warms our hearts and invites us to cherish sweet memories.

Christmas Luncheon

Just before Christmas, the sisters met at the Rainbow Grill, a restaurant where we had eaten often in our teenage years. We had lunch indoors on this cold December day, but in the 1950s and 60s we ordered and ate in our cars. At that time a car hop waitress took our orders and delivered our food. That was a big deal when we were younger.

The memories surfaced as we talked and laughed during lunch. We shared some of the senior moment pieces that the girls had sent to me, and I promised to read the rest of them at a later date.

We also discussed the meditations which Carol and I would like to use in the third part of the book. I asked them to please submit their pieces for the final section of the new book during the winter months.

After lunch, Sue rode with Carol and me to her house. When everyone arrived, we continued talking about the senior moments and then more seriously about the meditational pieces that the sisters would write for the new book.

It was imperative that the girls felt a part of this project, because their thoughts and words represent the group as a whole. Each sister shares a piece of our lives as we venture forward on our golden friendship journey.

Judy had inquired about the meditation part of the book in advance. She wrote her piece and asked if she could read it to the group. It was perfect. She read about counting her family's many blessings, and she shared a much-loved hymn, "Count Your Blessings."

Eight living Draco sisters, 2022

The sisters seemed motivated to participate in this project, which greatly encouraged Carol and me. We were hopeful that many of the sisters would soon submit their pieces to us so we could complete the final part of our story.

CHAPTER TWENTY-TWO

presentations and serious reflections

Florida Presentation

Carol and I were invited to present a book review at the United Church of Marco Island, Women's Fellowship Group in January of 2020.

We had done our preliminary preparation, and after we settled into our Florida condominiums for the season, we

First book review presentation

decided to drive over to the church to check the room where we would present.

We requested that they provide a park bench for us to sit on, and we also asked for microphones. It was a large hall. First there would be a potluck luncheon, and then Carol and I would do the book presentation.

As per usual, we stopped for a quick ice cream treat while we discussed last minute plans for the book review of *The Promised Piece.*

Once we finished our treat, Carol dropped me off at my condo. We were thrilled to prepare for our first book presentation. In fact, Chuck's relatives would be visiting at that time, so three of the women would attend the meeting, along with three of my local friends. We looked forward to having our own full table represented at the event.

Our Gift: A new year, a new beginning, and a fresh look at what is to come each day.

First Florida Presentation

Carol picked me up on the day of the presentation, and we were dressed like the cover of our book.

We drove to the church and met our friends. After the potluck luncheon, Carol and I put on our hats and sat on the park bench at the front of the room. Fifty women had gathered to hear the presentation, and a few men stopped by as well.

An hour was allotted to tell our story and to answer questions. We stayed on schedule, and the women seemed interested in our topic of forever friendship.

There were fun moments of our growing up years and sad moments regarding the death of my first husband at an early age and regarding Carol's stroke and rehabilitation. In conclusion, we explained that we planned to extend our book to include our present years, and we looked with expectation toward the future years to add to our friendship journey.

After a question-and-answer period, where the ladies were very interested to learn more about lifelong friendship, they thanked us for our presentation and invited us to come back to continue our journey in the future. We agreed to do that. Women purchased both paperback and hardback books before leaving that afternoon.

Meditations

We met at Mackle Park and picked a secluded park bench to discuss the direction that our new meditations project would take. Our sisters were beginning to send online personal pieces, which Carol and I enjoyed reading.

I read both Pastor Dale's and Donna's pieces aloud since they had just arrived. The messages spoke to our hearts.

Carol told me about the meditation that was on her heart to share in the book, and I shared what I was working on. We decided to remind the women to continue submitting their wonderful pieces.

Second Presentation

We were invited to give another book presentation to a P.E.O. meeting in March on Roger's Bay on Marco Island.

After driving to a lovely home, we were greeted by the women. Prior to the book review, we joined the group for a brunch.

This time we didn't have a park bench to sit on, but we were dressed in our "book cover clothing" complete with our hats and copies of *The Promised Piece*. We presented our friendship journey, answered questions, conversed with the women, and sold some books.

On the way home, we shared how comfortable we felt at this presentation. The women seemed to be interested in our topic of a friendship journey which included ten longtime friends. They were curious to learn more details about Carol and me personally, and they shared their friendship connections, as well.

Another presentation date for the upcoming 2021 season was added to our schedule.

Our Gift: Tomorrow is a new day, filled with promise, hope, and love.

Hammock Bay

The next encounter was worshiping at an Ash Wednesday Service which was held at our church, and then we enjoyed brunch on the island.

Upon leaving the restaurant, Carol and I drove to my condo where we parked the car and walked to the pond. We sat on a park bench to continue our conversation.

It was a lovely Florida day, and as we chitchatted, Carol noticed a movement in the water.

Her eyes got as big as saucers. We had a visitor coming to check us out.

A good-sized alligator was swimming toward the shore near us.

Instead of practicing our zigzag running skills, we moved to another park bench which was a distance away. After watching "Allie the Alligator" rest on the opposite side of the pond, we tried to get back into the swing of our conversation.

Aging Is Not Easy

Unfortunately, our prayer lists were becoming longer as more sicknesses, surgeries, and deaths had taken place. This was never a pleasant topic to discuss. However, it is a fact that as we age, death is even more imminent.

Our friend, Nancy, had lost her husband last June. Doug was our classmate and forever friend, and Nancy was grieving. She lives in Maryland, and her children and grandchildren live near her, except for her son who resides in Texas. She only occasionally returns to Grand Rapids where some relatives and friends still live.

We anticipated seeing Nancy in September at the sixtieth class reunion. Classmates were hopeful that she would fly to Michigan to join us for that event.

Other New Topics of Interest

Downsizing, senior home choices, health concerns, and making final decisions about our upcoming years are topics often mentioned during the present winter season of our lives.

Although aging gracefully can have its challenges, Carol and I decided to stay upbeat and remain as positive as we possibly can.

We walked back to my condo to read the manuscript about these topics before Carol left for home.

A Life Changer

When Carol and I entered my condo, Art was watching a program on television which was interrupted with a special news bulletin that the COVID-19 pandemic was sweeping across the United States.

The first patient in Florida had passed away from the mysterious coronavirus. Deaths were occurring all over the country.

The president of the United States appeared on television and announced that people must stay inside the U.S. borders and could no longer travel to other countries, nor could others travel to our country. The American borders were closed due to the spreading virus.

Art was glued to the television set as they continued giving the grim news. Masks must be worn in public places, and further mandates would be given from the governors representing each state.

Our conversation was over for the day. I walked Carol to her car. We waved and hugged as she left, and I quickly disappeared upstairs.

Many Changes Taking Place

There was a mass rush to stores to buy protective masks, latex gloves, hand sanitizers, paper products, and other household items. Trips to the grocery stores or drugstores displayed many empty shelves, a lack of certain products which were mandatory for daily living, especially recommended products for safety. People were hoarding products and certain foods as they feared a shortage. There was total uncertainty during the pandemic, with questions of how long it would possibly continue.

The world had suddenly changed, and people were notified on every form of media about the mysterious coronavirus. It seemed the virus started in a laboratory in China and was now spreading to every continent of the world.

Lockdowns, social distancing, and self-quarantine warnings were given. We were reminded to thoroughly wash our hands and use disinfectant sprays or wipes to clean surfaces that had been touched. These were daily warnings that were heard or read repeatedly on social media.

A Year Prior

One year earlier, we lived a normal existence and thought nothing of jumping into the car and going wherever we desired without a mask. Now we carried extra masks in our purses, pockets, and cars, along with hand sanitizers and even a pair of latex gloves just in case we needed them.

How much had the world changed? Were we more aware of social distancing? Did we turn down opportunities to be with people we longed to hug and hold? Could we withstand an undetermined amount of time living this way?

We preferred our freedom, especially with our family and friends. I thought back to a year earlier when Art and I arrived in Naples after a Christmas celebration with family near Charleston, South Carolina. Just days later, I received a text that the Jennings also arrived back in Florida after a two-week stay in Grand Rapids over the holidays.

Me: *Hey, Thelm, we are back at Hammock Bay, and I'm ready to meet for a park bench conversation ASAP! Love, Lou.*

Carol: *Hey, Lou. So happy you safely arrived.*

Me: *Art and I have been here for a few days... There is much to share. See you soon, Thelm.*

When we met, the conversation went back to the Draco sisters Christmas luncheon, followed by a dessert. Of course, this was still when we were carefree with few frustrations.

Our Gift: God has given us the gift of forever friends, whom we cherish.

Isles of Capri – COVID Restrictions

Our conversation at the Isles of Capri addressed the strangeness of life as the pandemic became the new focus of conversations.

It was our age group who was most at risk of contacting the viral infection. The focus was on the mature population (in the sixty and older age range) more than any other age group. Nursing homes and hospitals were full, and visitors were no longer permitted to see their loved ones indoors.

We had an emergency at the end of February. Art had been diagnosed with pneumonia and was taken to the emergency unit, where he was examined and tested. He did not have COVID but was on medication for pneumonia and housebound for two weeks inside our condo. This scared us, and we were extra cautious about staying isolated from others.

Pandemic Uncertainties

After talking about the uncertainty of a class reunion, we walked back to Carol's car. As we drove, we discussed the fact that our family members were not making plans to visit in Florida over spring break this year. Nobody was traveling far these days. People in Michigan were in lockdown mode, other than for essential things.

Before Art and I left for home in April of 2020, we dropped some grocery items off at the Jennings' condo. They planned to arrive in Michigan in June. We were masked as we stood a distance apart on their porch for a few minutes before leaving to travel north.

There was no touching, just a few words with sad hearts. Perhaps we would see each other in two months in Michigan. We had no idea if or when the governor would open up the state. We did know that it would be a strange summer, fall, and winter in our home state.

Although Carol and I could text and talk on the phone, it wasn't the same as personally meeting on our favorite park benches, having adventures, or enjoying ice cream together.

Our Gift: Life is a gift, and suddenly we began to appreciate things which had been taken for granted in the past.

Quarantining in Michigan

Art and I drove back to Michigan with hopes that things would be more normal. Florida was slowly beginning to open back up, but Michigan had extended their lockdown time.

Upon our arrival, we unpacked and talked with our children and grandchildren on cell phones and by text. We even Zoomed online with family and friends. However, there was not a living soul rushing over to see us in person. Children and grandchildren were protective of their parents and grandparents, and Art and I were pretty much quarantined for the first two weeks after we arrived home.

Our daughters had filled our refrigerator and cupboards before our arrival, and they continued buying our groceries and delivering them to our front porch. We finally insisted on doing our own essential errands.

We would walk in our neighborhood and stand a distance from the people we knew well, as we talked. We sat on a few front porches with masks on and maintained distance from the people we had missed so much over the winter months.

The children and grandchildren stopped over for Mother's Day in May and left a plant on our front porch. We gave each other air hugs from a distance, as they wished us special blessings and love.

There were two family birthdays in May. Our granddaughter had her tenth birthday. Our daughter had a drive-by party for Charlotte at their home. Relatives and friends decorated their cars and drove by, honking their horns as they yelled, "Happy Birthday, Charlotte!"

She sat in the front yard receiving gift bags and colorful balloons. We could only air-hug our granddaughter from a distance. Lawn chairs were spaced six feet apart as we conversed with family members.

The other party was an outdoor barbeque where we wore our masks and sat separated in my oldest daughter's front yard. Nine-year-old Padric opened his gifts, and we sang the birthday song. Masks were only taken off to eat, and then we waved and left the party without touching.

Carol called and described a couple of drive-by parties in Florida as well. We shared our experiences and realized that Florida was opening sooner than Michigan. Chuck and Carol were driving back to Michigan and would find a much different situation over the summer and fall months in the north.

CHAPTER TWENTY-THREE

what is happening now?

An Unexpected Adventure

Little did Carol and I understand that not all "Thelm and Lou adventures" are pre-planned, or even classified as positive experiences. Other than the windstorm six years ago, we had experienced fun and favorable Thelm and Lou escapades. But then everything changed. The normal enjoyable times we had previously engaged in, were not allowed to happen for a period. This was unknown territory for us, and we were not thrilled about the changes the coronavirus pandemic suddenly brought to our world in the 2020–21 timeframe.

Our regular park bench conversations were now non-existent, and our usual adventures were not even spoken about. Not only were we personally feeling tied down, but our wonderful country was experiencing a crisis.

The Dreadful Coronavirus

The deadly coronavirus that made its appearance in Asia and was now ravaging our nation.

People were contacting the virus and getting sick or dying. No one seemed exempt from the horrible coronavirus that had invaded our lives.

Early in 2020, COVID-19 became a challenge that affected the entire world. It caused people to stay isolated. More needed to be understood about this horrendous mystery virus, which was quickly moving to and through North America and elsewhere.

The news media reported that the coronavirus pandemic caused flu-like symptoms, attacked the lungs, and took the lives of people in every continent of the world.

Some Americans had received their yearly influenza injection, so they didn't initially pay much attention to the news media. They thought they were immune. However, as more COVID-19 cases were reported throughout various states, by February people were seriously listening and starting to wear masks as well as continuously using hand sanitizers.

Governors from many states mandated stay-at-home orders, suggesting physically separating from others and using masks when leaving the house. Washing hands thoroughly and often was highly stressed, along with the wearing of latex gloves at appropriate times. By maintaining social distance, people could protect themselves and others from the deadly virus.

Many people quarantined at home, while others were isolated in hospitals and nursing homes. Patients at these facilities could no longer have visitors. There was a shortage of ventilators available. Soon only emergency surgeries and COVID cases were the top priority at hospitals. There was a shortage of healthcare workers in some localities, and volunteers traveled to different parts of the country to serve where needed.

People were told to stay home in lockdown mode and to limit themselves by going to only essential places. The message was to use all safety precautions while purchasing groceries, getting medications at pharmacies, pumping gas, or personally being admitted at medical facilities.

Our Gift: Life surely wasn't following the footprint we had planned. But we shall keep doing our best at all times.

The New Normal

The new normal now included not only wearing masks and social distancing, but churches were closed, schools and day-care centers were suspended, and many employees had to work from their homes. Restaurants closed or offered only take-out or drive-up services, or they served at outdoor tables only which were separated by appropriate social distance.

This would continue until things began to slowly open according to guidelines from each state. Little did we know how long and to what degree these restrictions would last, depending on where people resided.

Trips Canceled

After years of being able to travel abroad, things changed, and many cancellations were made in an effort to remain healthy and safe from COVID–19.

Art and I had canceled a cruise to the Baltic in January when we heard about the coronavirus. The Jennings canceled their March transatlantic cruise in February due to the spread of the virus. It would not be safe to travel.

Although we were disappointed, we agreed that we would rather be in the United States during this deadly pandemic. We had no idea how the coronavirus would change the way things were done in our world.

The Jennings Arrived Home

When Carol and Chuck arrived in Michigan in June, there were restrictions at Cook Valley Estates whereby they could have no guests visit them at the big house where they now lived.

They were allowed to go to essential places to get take-out food, but basically, many places were locked down tightly in Grand Rapids.

Carol and I talked on our cell phones and sent online messages to each other and to our Draco sisters.

Is Different Good?

Churches, theaters, concerts, malls, beauty shops, exercise clubs, and almost all group activities were canceled or closed during the summer months. However, Carol and I met on a couple of park benches in Cascade and Ada as we continued to work on our book. We wore masks indoors and sat a distance from each other outdoors.

We talked about people spending more time working in their homes, while others supervised their children's online school lessons and activities. Because each state had a particular set of mandates to adhere to, it could get complicated.

Staying positive was the name of the game. Putting our faith and trust in God and praying that an inoculation would be discovered was our focus. We prayed that soon the COVID virus would be prevented from spreading.

We tried to keep our attitudes up and talked about what we could do to make the time go faster yet be productive in our own lives. Anger improved nothing. Instead, a positive attitude and maintaining our faith worked for Carol and me.

The pandemic restriction didn't stop us from enjoying a few ice cream treats during the summer. As we sat outside and distanced ourselves, we laughed and had a good time. Our philosophy dictated that we couldn't stop living.

Special Graduations

Events that had always been taken for granted as routine were no longer possible to do in 2020. High school proms were canceled, and many baccalaureate ceremonies and graduations were streamed. In most cases, only parents were invited to attend the ceremonies in a huge facility. Other schools held outdoor ceremonies.

Carol presented their grandson his diploma at the East Grand Rapids football field, and the Jennings family had an outdoor family party for Davis. He planned to attend Hope College in Holland to play football in the fall. This would depend on when contact sports would be allowed.

Art and I live-streamed our grandson Conlin's South Carolina high school graduation ceremony. We watched him present the high school valedictorian address online.

Months later, we celebrated with an outdoor party in Grand Rapids. He would be attending Clemson University in the fall.

Carol and I solemnly continued to pray for blessings on our grandsons, as they planned to pursue their college educations.

Up North during the Summer Months

Art and I went north to our cottage where we spent time in the summer months. Things seemed to be more open and relaxed in northern Michigan. Many annual festivals, parades, and wine-tasting events had been canceled for the summer. It was less busy, and we felt safer where fewer people congregated.

We also spent a few nights in Petoskey and visited friends who live in the Indian River area.

We met for lunch and sat a distance from Sally and Steve as we visited them at a large table.

Another way to stay in communication with friends was online Zoom meetings. It was a way to keep abreast of our lives with five couple friends who spend time together in Florida. It allowed us to talk in a group setting as we shared what was happening in Florida and Michigan.

Worship Services

Some churches live-streamed their services for over eighteen months. Many people felt more comfortable worshiping online in the safety of their private homes.

While certain churches were open in Michigan, others took a limited number of reservations, while others observed strict mandates. For instance, every other row of pews was roped off, with few people spread out per pew. Masks were worn, and Holy Communion was observed by partaking from portable foil packets. There were no hymnals or pew Bibles in place. Tithes and offerings were collected in baskets at the back of the sanctuary or online.

Congregants who chose to worship with the community inside of a church wore masks and sat a distance from others. There was no handshaking. Instead, elbow bumping, giving air hugs, or waves sufficed until things eventually got back to normal the following summer.

Coffee was served outdoors after church on a few occasions. Only purchased and wrapped cookies could be served. Nothing homemade was permissible.

Since there were many rules and regulations to adhere to, few weddings, funerals, social meetings, or parties were held indoors during the pandemic. Only a minimal number of people were allowed to attend these services or meetings if they were held indoors.

Meeting Diane Outdoors

Instead of meeting at a local coffee shop, this summer we met Diane outside at both Collins and Tassel Parks. It was safer to sit outdoors, and this would work until we could be together indoors. As our literary agent, Diane explained a new lead on a terrific publisher, and we presented her with a rough draft of our manuscript to edit.

Carol and I would work on Part III (The Future) of the book during the winter months in Florida. For as much as we had good intentions, we knew not whether we would have "together time" to sit on park benches in 2021.

It had been our original desire to conclude the book after the class reunion which was planned for September 2020. There was no class reunion. It had been postponed. Would there be a reunion a year later in 2021? That was the million-dollar question.

CHAPTER TWENTY-FOUR

historical happenings

Draco Sisters Precious Time

Carol and I discussed the fact that more people were meeting outside for social contact in 2020. In fact, when restaurants finally opened indoors at twenty-percent capacity, the Draco sisters started meeting for luncheons.

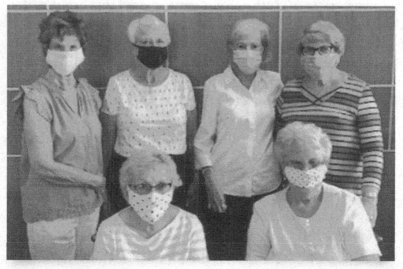

Draco gals masked for lunch

As a small group, we met over the summer months in a separate room at a restaurant, wearing our masks until we ate. Other times we met at the back of a restaurant and were seated at a huge table to maintain distance from other diners.

August Plans Postponed

The group planned to visit our friend, Sandy, in Holland. However, the year 2020 was an exception. Sandy's daughter, Susan, let us know the lockdown rules were in place at this time. A group of visitors was not allowed inside of the care facility. Rules stated that only two family members could visit outside for a short period of time.

We were disappointed that we could not see our friend.

Memories from 9/11/2001

The Draco sisters continued meeting for lunch during the summer and fall months. While enjoying our coffee, and dessert, we engaged in conversations, often remembering significant American events and dates from the past. As we celebrated Sharon and Carol's September birthdays near the anniversary of 9/11, the group remembered that event as if it had just happened yesterday.

I asked the sisters if they recalled where they were on September 11, 2001, nearly twenty years ago, and then inquired how they had felt on the day the Twin Towers in New York City were destroyed by terrorist suicide planes.

Sharon recalled that she had been on her way to work when she heard the startling news on the car radio. Later, when she arrived at work, she shared the bad news with her coworkers.

They turned on the television set and watched the video replay of both towers being destroyed by intruding airplanes.

Donna had been at work at a store. She wondered why so few customers were shopping that day. A phone call from her husband informed her regarding the reason why so few people were out and about.

Later, Donna and her husband attended an evening church service. They were with fellow worshipers, trying to make sense of this tragedy.

Sue worked with preschool children in an educational setting. She recalled an announcement over the intercom to staff members. They were told to turn off the classroom television sets. She learned later that this was an attempt to not alarm the young students about the grim news.

Carol and Chuck were celebrating her birthday on September 11 with a trip out east. They had spent the night in a Connecticut motel, and Carol had gone downstairs to get coffee. An emergency message was announced on a television set that the first tower had been hit in New York. She remembered that there was complete silence in the room. Hurried steps took her upstairs to their hotel room, where Chuck and she watched the second tower being demolished.

They left the motel and headed back home to Michigan. Few cars were on the highway.

There was no direct access to New York City, and phone calls were unable to connect during that time. Eventually, the Jennings reached their family members to inform them that they were heading home early from their trip.

"It was surreal, almost like a movie, instead of reality," Carol said.

Judy remembered that she was home baking banana bread. When her husband turned the television set on, it was then that they heard the alarming news. She recalled how hard it was to comprehend that this happened in America.

That day, I (**Marilyn**) was making an educational consultant visit at a school, and as I was walking down the hallway, I heard sobbing coming from an open classroom door. Of course, I went into the classroom to check the situation, not knowing about the New York disaster.

The young teacher had an educational channel on the classroom television set, when an emergency news bulletin reported the horrible event. The teacher turned the set off, but the students were upset, and they had many questions.

Everything happened so quickly. I went directly to the administration office to get some answers. The principal made an announcement to turn off all classroom technology. She said that she would come to each classroom to explain to the teachers why this was necessary.

Some parents of students, who were aware of the horrible news, came to pick their children up from school. They wanted their families together.

I made the decision to drive back to my office. The radio broadcast in my car gave an overview of the tragic events while I drove. When I arrived at my office, my coworkers filled me in on the details they had recently learned.

My colleagues and I watched reruns of the destruction caused by terrorist hijackers to the Twin Towers at the New York World Trade Center, the West Wing of the Pentagon in Virginia, and Flight 93 in Pennsylvania. Almost 3,000 lives were brutally lost that day.

Years later when the Draco sisters shared these remembrances, the room became quiet. After we voiced our feelings, we agreed about how empty we still feel when we relive tragic events in history.

Motivation: To pray for God's blessings
on our country.

Remembering JFK's Assassination: November 1963

The memories of when President John F. Kennedy was assassinated in Dallas, Texas, also surfaced. The feelings of hopelessness and disbelief that most Americans felt on that disastrous day were paramount in our minds.

The Draco gals were in their early twenties when the assassination took place. Most of us were working at our jobs when the unbelievable news first came across the radio and television media.

Weeks, months, and years later, books, newspapers, and magazine articles appeared, attempting to explain the horrific shooting and fatal death of our young president.

The women sat in silence for a while, thinking of where we were and what our thoughts had been at that time.

Judy shared that she was married and was home with her husband and young sons. She remembered the universal sadness and recalled that Jackie's wedding was scheduled that same Friday evening in November 1963.

Jackie was not at today's luncheon, so she couldn't share her emotions on the date of her wedding. However, Harvey and she proceeded with their plans that evening. They have been married for fifty-seven years.

Sue was living on an Army base in San Antonio, Texas, with her husband, Ron, and their baby daughter. They definitely remembered their feelings that fatal day. Ron had been serving his country in the same state where President Kennedy had been assassinated.

Sharon, Carol, Donna, and I were at work when we learned about the horrific assassination of our president. He and the governor of Texas were shot while riding in an open limousine during a Dallas parade.

Each woman present at the luncheon remembered the confusion as we waited to hear if our president would survive this tragic attempt on his life. The announcement came later that President John F. Kennedy had passed away in a Dallas hospital as the result of the gunshot wounds. What an impact it had on Americans!

Messages of sorrow were expressed from all over the world. Kennedy's widow, Jackie, their two small children, members of JFK's greater family, his cabinet, and all Americans felt deep emotion of unforgettable grief and disbelief regarding his death.

Sixty years later, we regret that President John F. Kennedy's life ended at the young age of forty-six. The mass media announced the arrangements for the funeral, which was broadcast in every household and business as the nation and world grieved.

CHAPTER TWENTY-FIVE

moving forward

A Final Seasonal Meeting

We decided to have one more park bench conversation before Carol and I departed for Florida in the fall of 2020. This final park bench conversation took place in Ada. We had lunch outdoors at Nonna's Restaurant on the porch and continued conversing after we drove to the park.

As much as Carol and I disliked the total lock-down in Michigan, our governor slowly allowed essential businesses to reopen. Recently, more places were opening with the wearing of masks at eateries, beauty shops, exercise clubs, and other shops. There were separation guidelines with fewer people allowed at establishments, with safety factors mandated.

Some churches were slowly allowing a small number of congregants to attend services and safety precautions were followed. Other churches chose to stay closed and present virtual services each Sunday.

Our church held Bible study and other group gatherings outdoors; even a communion service was offered when weather permitted. Church members brought their own elements to partake in the blessed sacrament of Holy

Communion as we prayerfully congregated together as the family of God.

It was the prayer of each church member to meet in the sanctuary, in a normal church setting with others. People who had always practiced freedom of religion, longed to worship and commune with other congregants.

Someday people will say, "Do you remember when the worldwide coronavirus restricted people from living their normal lives? Somehow, we survived."

Time for a Break

After walking the trails around the park and enjoying a lovely day, Carol and I located a picnic table in the shade, and we spread out a copy of our manuscript. We pieced together the events of the summer and then went for ice cream outside at Jam'nbean in Cascade. Laughter and fun could be heard from our table.

After Carol dropped me off at my home, I ran back to her car and motioned for the window to come down.

We smiled and in unison said, "See ya later, alligator; after while, crocodile."

Carol waved and backed out of the driveway, and I disappeared into the house, thinking ahead to our next park bench meeting in Florida.

The Next Chapter

As autumn approached, Carol and I set our expectations on traveling to Florida for the fall, winter, and spring months. We were excited to leave Michigan because a second wave of coronavirus was expected in the cooler months. Now our goal was to move to our Florida paradise before this occurred in the Midwest.

The rationale was that during the fall and winter months, we could walk the beach, sit on our lanai, eat outdoors, and attend church services in the Sunshine State. Outdoor activities such as golfing and boating were permissible, and small groups were allowed to gather at churches under extremely strict safety regulations. These were wonderful advantages for seniors living in Florida during the pandemic.

Art and I were the first to depart in early October for our southern destination. However, we decided to travel to upstate New York and stay on the Erie Canal on our way to the Sunshine State.

After enjoying the autumn fall colors, we traveled to Tennessee to visit our youngest daughter, Tiffany, and her family as well. Then, we continued to drive to South Carolina, where we visited our son, Todd, and his family, before heading to Florida for the winter months.

Art and I wore our masks and used much disinfectant as we stayed in various lodges and inns during our travels. The rooms were clean and separated and had been left empty for days between guests.

Carol and Chuck planned to arrive south the end of October.

October Florida Arrival

Both the Jennings and Emerys checked into our Naples, Florida, condominiums. Art and I planned to stay in Florida for nearly six months this season.

During COVID-19 we continued practicing safe habits. We mainly ate at outdoor restaurants, bought take-out food, and did a lot of home cooking. Other than going to church where safety mandates were practiced, we bought groceries, walked, and spent time on our condo lanai.

Art and I planned to leave Florida at the end of April. Carol and Chuck planned to return to Michigan in late May because their grandson, Kinzer, would be celebrating his thirtieth birthday, and a party was planned over the Memorial Day weekend. The children were also planning a fiftieth wedding anniversary celebration for Carol and Chuck in mid-June. Their usual routine was to travel home in June, but this year was different than it had been in the past.

Adventures on a Smaller Scale

In December, nine months after the coronavirus was announced, Carol and I found ourselves masked-up for our first mini-adventure in Florida. Because we couldn't experience a normal adventure, we created mini-adventures which would take just a few hours of our time.

We were excited to browse at a church Christmas bazaar with our masks on, and then we continued shopping at the Marco Walk Shops for Christmas presents.

At the end of our adventure, we stopped at Beebe's Ice Cream Shop where we sat on the park bench in front of the store and enjoyed our frosty treats.

Sadness

There was one heartbreaking piece of information that arrived that day. Our sister Sue's husband, Ron, had been hospitalized in Grand Rapids with coronavirus. Sadly, we received a message that he had been placed on a ventilator and had just passed away, only weeks before Christmas.

This disturbing news upset Carol and me greatly, especially because of our close relationship with this group of longtime friends. Ron's unfortunate death had happened quickly, and due to COVID, the funeral plans weren't immediately known.

We decided it was time to leave the bench we'd been occupying. We quietly walked back to our car in a more somber mood than when we had started out on our shopping adventure earlier that day.

Our Gift: Understanding that the Lord giveth, and the Lord taketh away, and trusting Him for guidance.

Carol and I grieved as we heard about the funeral arrangements which would take place at Fort Custer for Ron. The burial would be at the Michigan Military Cemetery, and only close family members would be in attendance.

Our hearts ached for Sue. No matter what age you are, losing a mate is a difficult period for the surviving spouse and the family. Christmastime would be especially lonely for them this year.

Carol added that it was tough to be away from our Draco sisters when death occurs, and because of the circumstances of COVID, it was even more difficult.

We discussed how we felt being away from Michigan, from our families, and our close friendship groups during the holidays. In the past, the Jennings flew home to Grand Rapids for the Christmas luncheon and family parties, and Art and I usually stayed in Michigan until January. This year, everything was different. 2020 was not a normal year. With the impending vaccinations, would 2021 be a better year?

Winter Holiday Celebrations

Michigan was on lockdown during the Thanksgiving and Christmas 2020 holidays. However, our daughter's family from Tennessee spent Thanksgiving with us in Florida. Our son's family visited us in Florida from South Carolina before the Christmas holiday. Our daughter, Allison, and her son, Newton, spent time with us after Christmas.

The Jennings children planned to fly to Florida in February and March 2021. It would be much safer to fly from the Midwest at that time of year.

Mentally, Carol and I were home in Michigan with our families and friends celebrating the holidays. However, physically, we were in the Sunshine State enjoying the nice weather accompanying the holidays.

Art and I were fortunate to have family with us before the holidays. Now we felt thankful for the blessing of being able to host Carol and Chuck for Christmas dinner. We attended the Christmas Eve service at church, and Carol and Chuck came for dinner on Christmas day. The four of us talked about the special meaning of the birth of the Christ child.

Our friends made the holiday season seem more normal for Art and me. We loved to entertain.

The beautifully decorated homes, along with the lighted boat show on Marco Bay, put us in a festive mood.

Florida Park Bench Visits

Carol and I met in several parks in Florida during the season. We met at Hammock Bay, Esplanade Marina, Isles of Capri, Plummer Park, the Yacht Club Marina, and finally on Caxambas Bay. We were determined to try and finish the book the following summer or fall. Regardless if there would be a reunion or not, we decided to conclude our second book in 2021.

Uplifting Conversations

After spending time together, Carol and I read the manuscript and made some decisions. We decided that we aren't angry because of the coronavirus. Instead, we are hopeful that soon most Americans will become vaccinated, and we looked forward with anticipation to the end of this horrible disease.

Each conversation started with the beautiful weather we were experiencing in Florida, along with the favor of being able to be together. We never wanted the pandemic nor the lives that were lost in the United States and abroad to be the focus of our conversation. Instead, we would speak of our children and our wonderful Draco sisters, all of whom we kept in touch with throughout the winter months.

Somehow, people adapted and made the best of a bad situation. Thanks to God for giving both Carol and me good health, along with patience, hope, and love. These characteristics helped us to stay afloat during the circumstances of COVID-19.

Park bench conversations wearing COVID masks.

CHAPTER TWENTY-SIX

mini-adventures

Vaccinations

Carol and Chuck had done the pre-registration work and were accepted at the Marlin's Stadium in Miami in late January 2021 for their first COVID vaccine. They returned three weeks later for their second dose and were happy to have completed the vaccines while sitting in their car in the stadium parking lot.

Art and I drove to Miami in mid-February for our first dose and then received our second dose in March. We were glad to be vaccinated in the Miami Zoo parking lot. It was a simple process to sit in our car, get inoculated, and wait fifteen minutes for a reaction check.

Fortunately, we were able to leave and travel back to Naples.

Most people wanted their family and friends to receive their vaccines with expediency. We had group plans with our friends for an Easter gathering after everyone became vaccinated.

However, we continued wearing our masks for added protection until told differently and followed safety guidelines as closely as possible.

Essential workers and the elderly population were vaccinated first. Then the plan called for compromised people with medical problems to follow. All adults under sixty-five years of age, and finally, all ages through twelve years old were offered the vaccine. The goal was to get the entire population vaccinated for the target of reaching herd immunity to eventually eradicate this horrendous coronavirus.

Many continued to pray that lives would stop being lost during the pandemic, and that people would be able to live life in a normal manner again. A percentage of people refused to be vaccinated. That was their choice at that point in time. Children under the age of twelve were still wearing masks for various indoor activities during the summer months.

Zoom Book Presentation

After the Jennings arrived in Naples, Carol and I were invited to give our first Zoom book review from her home office in Florida. Although it seemed impersonal and we preferred meeting in person, during the pandemic, Zoom meetings were the new normal. In times like these, people learn to make the best of each situation and accept the restrictions, as they hope for better times ahead.

Park Benches without Masks

Carol and I were thrilled to meet in parks and sit on opposite ends of park benches without our masks. Simply being in the presence of someone you appreciated was a wonderful occasion with or without a mask on.

Our first January conversation of the season was spent sitting on a bench looking for our favorite alligator in the pond. Although we didn't spot any action, we heard from a gentleman walking by that there is also a baby alligator living in the pond this year. Perhaps the larger alligator is a "she" instead of a "he," as we had thought last year.

Would the alligators make an appearance today?

Waiting to see the pond alligator

Fewer Travel Options

Carol and I talked about the fact that we were the only two couples from our Draco group who left Michigan this year for the winter months. The other couples who usually visited Arizona, Florida, and Georgia were no longer traveling this year.

Being close to home was imperative for many people due to illnesses, injury, and diseases which afflict seniors in their twilight years. Many preferred to be closer to families, local physicians, and medical facilities at home.

Plummer Park, Esplanade, the Yacht Club Marina

Carol and I continued having our park bench conversations at our favorite Florida spots. We never ran out of interesting topics of conversation. We looked forward to each meeting and of course the ice cream finales.

The Marco Island Yacht Club held a special luncheon and style show event which Carol and I attended with our friend

Sally, masked up of course. Afterward, we sat on a park bench to converse and enjoy the view of the boats at the Marco Island Marina.

Social Events Were Canceled

In Florida, there were no group holiday parties such as Valentine's Day or Saint Patrick's Day celebrations in 2021. The one party we attended was an outdoor tailgate party. The cars were distanced, and people brought their own drinks. Food was ordered, sanitarily wrapped, and delivered from a catering service. Homemade food was discouraged from being served in group settings.

It was wonderful to be together, even though we were spaced apart.

Naples Mini-Adventure

The next mini-adventure was a day spent shopping and then stopping at Starbucks for a warm drink on this cool and windy February day in Naples.

It had been a few years since we visited the Waterside Shops, which took most of the day.

> Being together was a cause for celebration in early 2021. We preferred having a near-normal mini outing over not being able to have any adventure at all.

We slowly ventured through many of the stores and galleries. It thrilled us to have the freedom to shop at a mall and order a Starbucks drink indoors.

Just to see other people and be allowed to shop was a huge moment for us to celebrate our mini-adventure. The masks and distance factors were taken for granted. Due to the present conditions, Carol and I were happy to have a half-exciting adventure. Being together was a cause for celebration in early 2021. We preferred having a near-normal mini-outing over not being able to have any adventure at all.

Whenever Thelm and Lou were together, another chapter was written about our life's journey, even though it seemed that complete normalcy was a thing of the past.

A Brunch Mini-Adventure

Before leaving Florida for Michigan, Carol and I decided to have one last mini-adventure in April. However, Carol had to handle a medical issue before we could enjoy the outing.

She has such stamina. Carol had pain in her right leg and could barely walk. Chuck took her to the emergency room at the Naples hospital for tests. She had a CT scan, and the doctor advised her to see an orthopedic surgeon because of a Baker's cyst behind her knee. He felt there was a possibility of having the cyst aspirated.

They made an appointment, and Carol saw the specialist. She received a cortisone injection to relieve the pain. Without delay after she left the doctor's office, she called me to make plans for a final mini-adventure.

We met on a Tuesday morning and drove to Skillets Restaurant for a lovely brunch. This was our first brunch adventure of the season and our last mini-adventure before departing Florida. We were going to savor each minute of our time together.

After eating, we drove through Marco Island and pulled into Caxambas Park overlooking the waterfront. We found a sleek white contemporary park bench where we sat watching some kayakers out on the water and birds flying over the pass.

We rushed to our car due to rain showers. Carol was walking well and wanted to stop at a women's sportswear apparel shop to browse. We found Sweet Annie's on the way home, where we enjoyed a special frozen treat to finish our mini-adventure.

Carol and I made plans the following Saturday night in Naples with our husbands for a lovely dinner at Truluck's Restaurant. We had waited until the last weekend in April to visit one of Art's and my favorite restaurants with our long-time friends.

a new chapter

Leaving Florida

Art and I would soon be driving home to Michigan to arrive the first of May, while the Jennings would return the end of May. We were excited about arriving in Grand Rapids and remained hopeful that this summer would be better than last year.

In the middle of May 2021, a presidential announcement was made that after being vaccinated twice and after the three-week waiting period, Americans could stop wearing masks under certain conditions. It was May before some governors allowed the discarding of masks, but it was also suggested to keep masks available to wear when necessary.

> Being able to adapt is the name of the game in times like these.

Michigan Arrival

A day after arriving home, Art packed and flew to Texas to visit his daughter who had surgery. He stayed with Allison at her new home as she recovered.

I spent Mother's Day with our Michigan family where I enjoyed a nice Sunday with loved ones. It was time to organize for a beautiful Michigan summer.

Carol and Marilyn Reunited

Carol and Chuck arrived home from Florida the first week in June 2021. Although Carol and I spoke on our cellphones and text messaged for several months, we finally got to meet and have a face-to-face park bench conversation in Grand Rapids in June. Our Ada Park bench conversations are always special because of the beauty of the pond, hiking paths, picnic area, and many athletic fields.

Today we saw a group of teenagers swinging on separate hammocks, chatting, and making the most of their social distancing time together during the pandemic. Being able to adapt is the name of the game in times like these.

There was an abundance of topics for Carol and me to share. Art and I had been home for six weeks, and now Carol and I could finally meet in person. Although we had our trusty masks with us, we sat at opposite ends of the park bench and enjoyed the warmth of the sunshine without masks. We got ice cream after we worked on the manuscript, a great reward for being productive.

Graduations

Later in June, our family celebrated an outdoor graduation party in Grand Rapids for Conlin, whose graduation we had missed due to COVID in 2020.

Our granddaughter, Karlin, graduated from high school in June 2021 and was accepted at Clemson University where she joins her brother, Conlin, who will be a sophomore in the fall.

It is Art's and my hope to visit our grandchildren on campus when COVID is no longer a threatening factor.

A Special Celebration

In mid-June, Carol and Chuck celebrated their golden wedding anniversary in Michigan.

We had talked about being married for fifty years and remarked that we remembered our parents celebrating this special anniversary some years ago. Now Carol and Chuck had arrived at this magical golden number.

Their son, Scott, with his wife, Susan, and their sons hosted a Friday outdoor dinner at their home in Norton Shores for Carol and Chuck.

Jennings family celebrating a special fiftieth wedding anniversary

A private dinner with eighteen family members at the historic Lilley Mansion in Spring Lake was held on their actual anniversary date on Saturday evening, June 19. Their children hosted the dinner on this milestone anniversary date at this special bed and breakfast site. Their gift was an overnight for Carol and Chuck and included breakfast on Sunday morning.

Carol said that a toast was made before dinner on Saturday evening. She later gave a speech between the entree and dessert courses. Her heartfelt presentation was a surprise to everyone.

> As an only child, Carol never dreamt that she would have such a large and beloved family.

Apparently, Carol woke up in the middle of Friday night with the idea of giving a speech at the family dinner. She got up and wrote out her ideas. She kept it a secret until she made the announcement Saturday evening at the dinner.

Carol addressed each one of the family members who were present, which included their three sons, their wives, the grandchildren, and their dates.

After she presented the personal messages, she gave a final thanks to all and revealed her feelings of love for each one present.

There were tears and hugs. Later their granddaughter, Kailey, framed her grandmother's speech notes and presented it to her as a gift. This was a remembrance of the golden wedding anniversary, which meant the world to Carol.

Additional nights were spent at the Spring Lake Holiday Inn for the traveling family members. There were so many fun moments at this celebration that the family will never forget.

A Future Trip

As Carol told me about her weekend, the joy on her face reflected how pleased she was to have celebrated their anniversary with loved ones. As an only child, Carol never dreamt that she would have such a large and beloved family.

Chuck and she also planned a transatlantic trip in 2022 to celebrate their anniversary if conditions enabled them to travel at that time. After canceling several trips due to the pandemic, they were hopeful that they would be able to take this trip out of the country next year. It would be a final memory of their special anniversary.

Impending Class Reunion

Our sixtieth class reunion had initially been the target date to complete our book in September of 2020. Now, we decided to wait and see if the vaccination would bring the healing which our nation so desperately hoped for.

Carol and I decided that we would conclude our story after the reunion, a year later than we had initially expected. We hoped and prayed that this plan would come to fruition.

Marty and I met in June with personnel at the Railside Golf Club where the reunion would potentially be held in September 2021. Carol had a summer meeting at her place, and four of the committee members met at the club in September to finalize plans for the reunion. It was our hope that the event would happen this year, and that a decision would also be made to meet for yearly luncheons in lieu of dinners starting next year in 2022.

Meeting Friends

After meeting with the Draco sisters at a restaurant for a luncheon in Byron Center, we had a tour of our sister Donna's new senior living home in June. The women sat in an open area and enjoyed a cool drink, as we talked and planned a date to visit our friend Sandy in Holland.

Judy checked to see if the group could visit Sandy indoors at the care center. After making the necessary calls, we learned that the vaccinated women will be permitted to visit our friend in the larger fireplace room in July.

Holland Visit

The sisters drove to the care home to visit our friend Sandy at the memory unit. We wore our masks in the lobby until we filled out paperwork and had our temperatures taken. As a group, we visited Sandy in the fireplace room where she sat in her wheelchair and sweetly smiled.

After talking to Sandy's daughter, Susan, and to Bob, Sandy's husband, we left to eat lunch at a Holland restaurant. Bob joined us.

Our Lake Adventure

Carol and I decided to go to northern Michigan to spend a few days at my Lake Leelanau cottage with our husbands. Our intent was to have our cover picture taken and to read the manuscript while overlooking the lake. We wanted to make sure that we had included everything in our book on our journey thus far.

We had been on this same cottage adventure in 2015 when the straight-line windstorm occurred. It was highly unlikely this would ever happen again. However, after the 2020-21 pandemic, we understood how quickly unexpected situations can occur.

Besides taking photos wearing our trademark hats, we sat on a park bench which overlooked a sparkling northern lake and enjoyed the nature around us.

After multiple park bench conversations and having fun regular and mini- Thelm and Lou adventures, we were ready to take a break to do some serious thinking about our next journey into tomorrow. For now, Carol and I strive to do our best while living in the present, by staying focused on today. However, our thoughts are to start reflecting more on the eternal domain after this project is concluded.

Following our photo shoot, the four of us took time for dinner in Fishtown and we also enjoyed ice cream, of course.

Our Gift: Show love and pray for each other because there are many uncertainties in life.

Forever Friendship Piece:

Friendship Memories – Jackie (Ainsworth) Seinen

Thinking back over sixty-plus years is difficult. A few of my friends are the same ones I had in kindergarten at Godfrey Elementary School. I added more when our class combined with classes at Lee High School in the eighth grade.

Our high school years were a special time of growing and of spreading our wings with our Draco sisters. I was so blessed to have bonded with girls having like moral values, and a love of God. We had good clean fun together. But now that we are experiencing the golden years, some of the LHS sisters are having health issues, and after losing one of our special Draco friends to cancer, it seems like I want to hold on more tightly to every moment.

Certain of God's promises, we know that we will continue to be together with new bodies in the eternal life. What a glorious day that will be. Our friendship group will live on with the most awesome Friend known!

Thank you for helping me remember and for being such great friends.

Jackie has always been a sweetheart and fun to be around. She has a very endearing personality. She played the trumpet in the school band and later became a nurse. Jackie was married

235

to Harv. They had a very close relationship and a Christian family. Harv had surgery with follow-up treatment at Mary Free Bed Rehabilitation Hospital. After he received chemotherapy and radiation treatments, Jackie was his caretaker. He was later put into hospice care at home and recently passed away. Our prayers are that God will be with Jackie and her family at this time.

Undetermined Factors

Carol and I were trying to make a date to read our manuscript and to eventually decide with our reunion committee regarding our 60/60 class reunion. Would the class reunion be held this September? It was Carol's and my initial projection that our book would be completed after the September 2020 class reunion, but now we remained uncertain if the reunion would be held one year later.

Another concern was with regards to COVID-19 booster shots which were recommended for our age group first. It seemed that compromised people could get injected sooner than the eight-month projected waiting period. Would the Delta or Omicron variants cause problems in the fall and winter months? Should all those twelve years and older get the booster?

Would the reunion possibly be postponed until 2022?

Becoming More Mature

It is a fact that everyone is becoming more mature each day. Life keeps moving forward.

Therefore, it makes sense to remain grateful and stay connected with family and longtime friends. It also makes sense to eat healthy, exercise regularly, and most importantly, maintain our faith, which gives true peace, contentment, and purpose.

Each year as we light an additional birthday candle, Carol and I are thrilled to add more park bench conversations and adventures to our lifetime friendship journey.

Impacting the Lives of Others

Whenever we read or hear book reviews of our friendship story, we realize our story has caused other women to reach out and contact their friends from the past. A phone call, a text, or perhaps a copy of our book is sent to a friend or to a group of friends which inspires a reconnection between them. And *this* inspires us too.

Five K-12 sisters' last visit with Sandy, before her death

CHAPTER TWENTY-EIGHT

many changes taking place

Blessings Are Needed

As health issues became more prevalent in our group, Carol and I intended to be extremely sensitive about health problems included in our book.

Four of the Draco sisters had become widows. I had led the way in 1994, but I am currently remarried. Nancy lost Doug in 2019 and Ron, Sue's husband, passed away from the coronavirus in 2020. Jackie's husband, Harv, passed away in September 2021.

The only sisters to pass away to date, have been Marcia in 2012 and Sandy in 2023.

Currently, we have had one stroke survivor, five of the women have survived cancer, two of our sisters have dementia, and recently another sister was diagnosed with kidney disease.

Several of the men have had prostate cancer or other forms of cancer. A few husbands now have heart stents, one husband is connected to a feeding tube, another broke his hip, and one has COPD.

In September 2021, we were notified that Jackie's husband in hospice care had passed away.

As a group, we attended Harv's funeral.

Prayers were being lifted for our entire family, that God may bless and keep each Draco sister healthy, along with all our beloved mates.

Generations

Art and I are great-grandparents as of July 2020 to baby boy, Asher Alan. Carol and Chuck followed us when their grandson and his wife had a baby, Charles Joseph, in November 2021.

They made advance plans to fly home for Christmas to be in Grand Rapids so they could meet their first great-grandson.

We talked about baby showers, births, baptisms, birthday parties, and all the celebrations that we hope to experience in the future. In addition, we both have younger grandchildren who are in K-12, college age, and married grandchildren.

Motivation – Family visitations bring pure happiness and joy to all involved.

Sister Time

My older sister, Joanie, younger sister, Marcia, and I (the middle sister) met up north in North Port for some special time together in September. As we walked the beaches of Lake Michigan, shelled, took sunset pictures, and enjoyed dinner together at Fisher's Tavern, we enjoyed our precious sister time.

It was important to be together, especially after losing our sister, Jan, earlier in the summer. None of us had gotten to tell our sister good-bye since her death happened quickly, and we felt bewildered.

Joanie's husband had passed away, and Marcia's husband presently lives in a care home. We needed sister time to process everything that had recently happened.

Our parents are gone, so we have each other to cherish and to share with. Together the three of us try to comprehend family issues. We understand each other because we grew up together, and it is with much gratitude that we spend time with and appreciate our dear sisterhood.

Senior Sisterhood

Having a blood sister is most satisfying. I was blessed to have three sisters. The remaining three of us still have a close relationship. We enjoy sister time, conversations, lunches, travel, and the contentment of knowing we are loved by each other.

Our parents have been gone for several years; however, our youngest aunt is still living and resides in California. We have many cousins and nieces scattered across the country as well.

Somehow, a feeling of sisterhood remains despite the distance.

As we age, sisterhood becomes more important to us. We desire to hold on to the memories of the past as we anticipate the future years. Getting together to share our lives with other interested sisters gives women a feeling of completeness. Sharing ideas, thoughts, creative interests, spiritual reflections, our blessings, and our worries are all part of the sisterhood bond.

Final 2021 Luncheon

One more gathering was held in October, before I left for the season. After the luncheon in Hudsonville, we were invited back to Judy's condo for dessert. Judy resides near the restaurant, and it was a lovely afternoon.

It was the final luncheon of the year for me. I will not see my Draco friends until May. Carol will join the sisters to celebrate a Christmas luncheon in Grand Rapids.

The three Lutke sisters enjoying time together

Deaths

Several significant deaths occurred after my younger sister, Jan, suddenly passed away in June. My cousin died in July; my stepmother and Harv Seinen (sister Jackie's husband) passed away in September; and then a longtime neighbor was called home in November. In December, my longtime colleague, Sue, suddenly passed away in Florida. Carol, our friend, Vicki, and I had lunch with Sue just weeks before her death.

Within the same timeframe, a friend of Carol and Chuck's suffered a brain aneurism; she also passed on to her eternal home.

At that time, we had funerals to attend, and grief to deal with. Both Carol and I were feeling blue. Our family and friends units were upset, and we found it impossible to reflect and write for several weeks.

Our Gift: Turn your prayers heavenward and make your prayers the voice of faith turned Godward.

Goals and Timelines

When Carol and I decided to write a second book, we thought the process would go much faster than it actually went. We have learned that our goals aren't always achieved on the timeline which we initially anticipated.

We thought our fine-tuned outline would be followed closely, and the conclusion of our story would take place after the class of 1960 held our reunion in September 2020.

Whenever the years 2020-2021 are mentioned, people understand that things changed during those years. Carol and I learned that the blueprint for solid planning, which we used for our intended master plan, was impossible to follow.

Lesson: Never think that things will go smoothly and as planned. They definitely will not, but keep the faith.

One Last Summer Adventure

Carol had an appointment in Spring Lake, so we decided to have one final adventure in Michigan prior to leaving for Florida.

She picked me up in the morning, and we enjoyed a brunch at the Village Baker Restaurant in Spring Lake. Then we rushed to Carol's afternoon appointment just blocks away.

I made some phone calls until Carol appeared with a short, new stylish hairdo. We drove to the Grand Haven channel area where we parked the car and walked from the channel to the pier overlooking beautiful Lake Michigan.

Memories of yesteryear surfaced as boats traveled through the channel, and people were seen slowly strolling along the picturesque pier. The red lighthouse could be seen in the distance.

We watched a group of young people taking group photos, and others were diving into the warm August waters of Lake Michigan. As we observed, we also recalled being the same age as this group. Was it that many years ago?

Then, we walked back to a park bench along the channel and got comfortable. We heard chatting as we people-watched in the sunshine on this gorgeous fall day.

Carol had lived in the lake front area for several years, and she felt very comfortable at this location. We probably could have spent more time sitting on the park bench, but it was time to travel back to Grand Rapids.

When others walked by with ice cream and snow cones, we strolled to our car and prepared to drive to a local ice cream shop where we purchased a tasty treat for the drive back to Grand Rapids.

LHS 2021 Class Reunion

On the evening of the reunion, forty classmates met at the Railside Golf Club. After registering, the Lee High School class of 1960 met for a social cocktail hour before dinner.

When seated at tables, classmate and committee chairman, Marty Reynolds, gave a welcome speech. Reverend Dale Kronemeyer offered a prayer before the waitresses served beautifully presented, pre-ordered, plated meals in the dining room.

After dessert, a "Memory Moments Program" followed which included a welcome to classmates from seven states: Arizona, Georgia, Indiana, Maryland, Michigan, New Jersey, and Texas.

When I inquired at the beginning of the program if this was Rebel Country, the class of 1960 unanimously answered, "Yes, we definitely are still Lee High Rebels."

A PowerPoint presentation of yearbook senior pictures was presented by Rev. Dale. The names and dates of our departed classmates' deaths were shown on a digital screen. The guests offered positive and fun memories while reminiscing about our deceased friends from the past. The bond between our Lee High School class of 1960 is as strong as ever.

We also remembered administrators and teachers who were special to our class. This gave classmates an interactive time to speak, share, and focus on both nostalgic and humorous memories from yesterday.

The idea of changing from dinner to luncheon reunions in the future was introduced and well-received by the classmates.

Many interacted during the program and listened as I read pieces from a poem written thirty years ago by classmate, Tom Zuidema. It recalled that we are "Still Rebels, After All These Years Together."

Eloquent words were shared which our departed classmate, Doug Greenwold, had written in *The Promised Piece* a few years ago. Not a sound could be heard as Doug's words echoed in the room that evening.

We also recognized Mr. Bob Wright, a favorite teacher, coach, and deceased friend of the class. The 1960 Echo yearbook had been dedicated to Mr. Wright, a man who typified the Rebel spirit at Lee High School.

Classmates stayed and continued socializing before leaving for home. Even though our numbers were less than hoped for, the class of 1960 had their twelfth five-year class reunion (one year late). This gives us hope for the future years that good friends will keep on meeting, caring, and sharing.

Motivation: For special friends who inspire each other to maintain our memories to keep our forever friendship dreams alive.

The reunion committee was thrilled that the evening had been a success. Several of our classmates and their mates expressed that they truly enjoyed themselves. It gave everyone added joy to be able to meet this year after a year of interruptions. In fact, several months later, classmates still complimented this reunion. Many said it was the best reunion that they had attended over the sixty-one-year history of the class of 1960.

When anticipated events are postponed, people are disappointed. However, under the circumstances, the class of 1960 was excited to be together, and we look forward to many more reunions in the future.

PART III

heartfelt meditations
(the future)

purpose

CHAPTER TWENTY-NINE

prayerful moments

Setting Goals

As Carol and I look forward to the *future* years, we realize that each day has purpose, and we must live in the here and now. We must take baby steps and enjoy each day at a time, with the intent of fulfilling God's purpose for our lives.

Our discussions often lead us to the topic of making short-term and long-range goals as retirees. We realize that we won't live forever. However, we talk about expectations and activities that we still can achieve. Our goal is to be physically able to actively participate in everyday life for some years to come.

It seems to us that short-term goals are more attainable and more doable to plan at this stage of our lives. If for some reason these short-term expectations need to be altered or canceled, we might not be quite as disappointed.

Although it is best to establish goals, we realized that human plans are made to be changed or broken. Only God's eternal plan truly matters.

Carol and I talked about our relationship with God when we met, and we reflected on spiritual meditative moments during our senior years of life.

As we focused on the last chapters of this book, we thought about the "meditation chapter" of our friendship story. We felt an extra-close relationship with God, our churches, our families, and our friendship base.

Motivation: To focus on our future with a song in our hearts.

Be Truthful, Strong, and Ready to Face Challenges – Carol Jennings (as told to Marilyn Emery)

Be Truthful with Yourself: Carol explained that people must live their lives and be truthful about what they wish to accomplish while on earth. It is important to be honest with ourselves about where we personally are at this particular time, especially for those in the winter season of their lives.

She said, "When being truthful with ourselves, we realize that as we enter the senior-citizen phase of life, our bodies have become somewhat limited in what we can do physically. We tend to think twice about our activities and where we care to travel. For instance, instead of overdoing and then aching later or going someplace and later wishing we hadn't gone, we just don't do it."

It is a fact that our age group is collectively classified in the "senior" or "elderly" category. That fact hits us square in the face. For example, the deadly coronavirus that took many lives worldwide in 2020-21 and beyond, targeted older people who were already compromised and had additional physical problems. Unfortunately, their immune systems are weaker. This age group included us. Carol and I agreed that we must be truthful with ourselves because truth has a way of defining us no matter what age we may be.

I responded with, "We may think, *Who us? Who me? Not our age group! The time went by far too quickly, and there is more we still want to accomplish. There are places to go, projects to finish, songs to sing, people to visit, talents to use, and books to read (or write). Surely the statistics must be talking about someone else.*"

But the facts are true. When we look at life through the lens of truthfulness and accept these facts, we are included in the golden generation, the "venerable" who are revered and respected at this advanced stage of our lives.

A big chuckle followed as we tried to use positive words for the elderly and at the same time remain somewhat truthful. But what really counts is that we know *God is the way, the truth, and the life* (John 14:6 KJV) no matter what age we are now or live to be. Indeed, what a comfort that is. We feel secure in Jesus' words which stated that "*no man cometh to the Father, but by me*" (John 14:6 KJV).

Our Motivation: By having faith in God, we can do all things through Him who gives us strength.

Be Strong: Carol explained that the second characteristic is that of being strong and diligent, as we still make decisions for ourselves in the present … and for the future years.

"Inner strength is pertinent as we face decisions regarding adult housing, our health, financial and religious choices, and even death," Carol stated.

At this present stage of life, we should choose to be strong and full of courage. Carol and I discussed this and declared, "It's much easier said than actually done!"

Be Willing to Face Challenges: Carol talked about the final point of facing challenges, which is difficult to handle, especially in the golden years of our lives. These challenges are often unknown to us, and we must be ready to accept whatever happens in life. For instance, issues we must face in a brave manner are serious family issues, making difficult choices, and even the bad news which may confront us.

We summarized that no matter what happens in the future, we must remain truthful and strong as we face the challenges that come our way in our twilight years.

CHAPTER THIRTY

heartfelt meditations

Reflections

Judy had asked in advance about writing her meditation, and she agreed to read it to the group at our Christmas dessert gathering at Sue's home.

After Judy read her meditation, the other women started submitting their pieces. We were thankful for their heartfelt messages.

Count Your Many Blessings – Judy Walkotten

One of my favorite hymns is "Count Your Blessings." Because my very special husband, Rich, and I have celebrated over sixty years of marriage, we have had many blessings to be thankful for and to celebrate over the years. The biggest blessing is that Jesus Christ gave His life for us, so we can confess and worship Him as our Savior and Lord. We look forward to being with Him in heaven someday.

Over two years ago, Rich was put on a permanent feeding tube for twenty-four hours per day ... for the rest of his life. As an only child, I am simply amazed that we have sixty-four members in our family. All these members have made us feel totally blessed. It is not that we have escaped suffering heartaches throughout our lives. We have three grand babies that were buried, and other grandchildren have survived serious illnesses. The Walkotten Family counts our many blessings, as we give thanks to God for the miraculous works that He has done.

The Lord Is the "Great I Am" – Jackie Seinen

A devotional that I read touched my heart during the worldwide pandemic of 2020 which caused havoc in our lives. We were extremely blessed because we knew who was in control of our lives. The Lord had our attention during that time. He is the Great I Am! In such times, we must pray and seek God's guidance and wisdom.

God protects us always—from conception, through our growing years, and even now after we retire, and our bodies are wearing out. From the beginning to the end, God is there, right beside us, leading us all the way. Through joy and happiness, the Lord is there. Through pain and stress, He never leaves us or forsakes us.

Our creator can do anything. There is no problem too big for God. The Great I Am rescues, sustains, and gives us peace that passes all understanding.

In the future when God makes all things new, we will be free from mourning, pain, and death. He is the Great I Am, who is in total charge. When the battle is done and the victory is won, our Lord will carry us through.

Leaning on Jesus – Marilyn Emery

As I was pondering my meditation for the conclusion of *The Power of Friendship,* the song, "Leaning on the Everlasting Arms," came to mind. The words fellowship, joy divine, blessed peace is mine, and being safe and secure from all alarm, brought me to the realization that our lives are always in the Lord's hands. We have nothing to dread or fear when we are leaning on the everlasting arms of Jesus. This brings blessed assurance to my soul.

When we meditate, think deeply, and engage our minds in the Holy Word, we have joy, peace, and security, as we lean on our beloved Lord. His strong shoulders and hands are available to us. He promised to be with us always, while carrying us through the joyful times as well as the broken times of our lives. He will lead us back to the fold and protect us forever.

I find as a retiree that I have more time to pray, read, study, and focus on the Scriptures.

These precious moments provide a marvelous opportunity to meditate in solitude, to pray, and to find God's purpose through His Word for my life.

Living through the pandemic, I realize that fear and anxiety have no place in our lives.

Although it was unlike any disaster most of us have ever experienced in our lifetime, we still were secure in knowing who was ultimately in control of everything.

Jesus told us not to fear nor be afraid 365 times in the Bible. Therefore, we must bring our needs to Him in prayer and learn to lean on Him completely. This will bring comfort and reassurance while restoring us to regroup and journey onward.

When we lean on Jesus, we feel His peace and contentment knowing that our heavenly Father will take care of our every need.

Our Motivation: To have faith in our hearts, as we look forward with hope to the future.

In the 50s – Sharon VandeGevel

In the 1950s, we weren't hit with the peer pressure to do drugs, get drunk, or live with a boyfriend, thankfully. It would have certainly changed the whole dynamics of our high school days. We were so naïve.

Most of our free time was spent at family, church, or school events. In the summer, we mixed it up a bit by going to the beach to waterski or to just try to get a tan. Our lives weren't exciting, but we always had fun.

The underlying theme was that we were all raised as Christians, and religion was the groundwork in the lives of all our families. We knew the Bible, could sing the words to all the old familiar hymns, and worked to give ten percent of our less-than-high incomes to the Lord. We even prayed before meals, all this while attending public school, where we were still allowed to pray without fear of being taken to court.

In contrast, twenty years later (after God was kicked out of anywhere but church), I worked in a public high school office. We had students who worked with us during their free hours. One day, a group of kids were talking about a party somebody was going to throw the following weekend. They were planning what they were going to drink. One of them asked me about the partying and drinking that I might have done in the "good old days." I told them that we didn't drink at all. They did not believe me. I also said that we didn't do drugs and barely knew what marijuana was. They emphatically didn't believe that either. I felt sorry for them.

These students were dealing with more negative problems than we did in our day, granted.

But I couldn't help but believe that if God were welcomed back into the public schools, we could wait with expectancy to see what blessings He would arrange for us from start to finish.

256

The Lord Is My Light – Donna Tillema (as told to Marilyn Emery)

Donna loves to worship the Lord by singing in a church choir, and for several years, she also sang in a women's trio. She mentioned hearing a song based on Psalm 27 referring to not being afraid because the Lord is our light and salvation. The church choir in which she sang, practiced the hymn, "The Lord Is My Light." It was not her favorite song in her younger years. The choir director had the group practice it over and over again.

Interestingly, during the gray stay-at-home days of the pandemic as well as other difficult times, she has found these words ringing in her head.

Donna said, "Singing this hymn brings me comfort and has become a favorite of mine. I sing it often and reflect on the words as I meditate on God. Now the song gives me peace in times of darkness and fear because I desire to live in God's presence each day of my life. I call upon Him because it refreshes me, gives me hope, and teaches me to trust in the Lord always. He is my light and my salvation."

A Sweet Story – Nancy Greenwold

As I stand at the seashore, a ship at my side spreads his white sails to the morning breeze and starts for the blue ocean. He is an object of beauty and strength, and I stand and watch him until at length, he hangs like a speck of white cloud just where the sea and the sky come down to mingle with each other. Then someone at my side says: "There! He is gone."

Gone where? Gone from my sight—that is all. He is just as large in mast and hull and spar as he was when he left my side and just as able to carry his load of living freight to the place of destination. His diminished size is in me, not in him; and just at the moment when someone at my side says, "There! He is gone," there are other eyes watching him coming, and other voices ready to take up the glad shout, "There! He comes!"[2]

Nancy stated that the song the family and friends sang at her husband's funeral approximately two years ago was, "It Is Well with My Soul." It was chosen by her daughter, Sarah, and Nancy for the small intimate service before the larger funeral. It was perfect, and the words will never be forgotten.

The hymn speaks of peace like a river, sorrow like sea billows roll, all praise to the Lord for dying for our sins, faith shall be sight beyond the scroll of clouds, and concludes: "The trump shall resound, and the Lord shall descend, even so, it is well with my soul."

Rest in peace, dear Doug. Many are looking forward to rising in glory to meet our God and be reunited with you in the future. "It is well with my soul, it is well, it is well with my soul."[3]

Our Motivation: Don't cry because it is over. Smile because it was. Shalom

---

Some Reflections Regarding Life and Eternity – Rev. Dale Kronemeyer

As I am writing these thoughts, our world has been turned upside down due to the coronavirus (COVID-19) that has already taken the lives of over seven hundred thousand people in the United States and over four and a half million people worldwide since the last count.

---

2   Luther F. Beecher (1813-1903), Gone from Sight, (Often attributed to Henry Van Dyke)
3   "It Is Well with My Soul," written in 1873 by Horatio Spafford and composed by Phillip Bliss, was first published in Gospel Hymns No. 2 by Ira Sankey and Bliss (1876)

I would like to begin with addressing the subject of fear. As a young child, I was taught a prayer that addressed the greatest fear of young and old alike.

> Now I lay me down to sleep, I pray Thee, Lord,
> my soul to keep. If I should die before I wake,
> I pray Thee, Lord, my soul to take.

Often, I thought this to be a strange prayer for a young child to say every night before going to sleep. In today's world, parents are not as likely to talk about such a topic, but for us World War II babies, death was not an avoided subject. Not since Pearl Harbor and World War II that took the lives of over four hundred thousand Americans has the fear of death been so real.

My classmates from the Lee High School class of 1960 may have a few memories of their fathers leaving for war, (mostly from pictures we have seen) and our moms raising us alone in those days, praying often that God would bring our daddies home alive. At the end of the above prayer there was usually a tag, "God bless Daddy, Mommy...."

I do remember the Christmas of 1945, just before my fourth birthday, my father arrived home from that terrible war. Our early years were lived in the "shadow of death." Once again that shadow is real whether it is from living during a time of a pandemic or just getting older.

Currently we have about a third of our classmates that have already passed from this earth to their eternity. As we get older, that children's prayer is a lot less about the very remote possibility of "if I should die" to the adult prayer of faith, "Lord, it won't be too long now before you take me to my heavenly home."

As I approach the age of maturity, my peace comes from my faith in God. My faith rests in the promise of God that if I place my trust in Jesus, who died for my sins and conquered death when He rose from that grave over two thousand years ago, I too would conquer the grave and receive eternal life.

Of course, I wonder often how much more time I have on this earth and wonder how my death will happen, but it is more important to remember the wonderful things that this life has given to me. I carry with me the glorious promise that our heavenly home is a place where there will be no more sorrow, sickness, or pain.

Part of handling all the fears we face in this life, is the trusting of the same God to carry us through the entire journey of life.

For most of us, the blessing of family is what gives us our greatest joy, but another thing that brings me so much joy is the bond I still have with those who were classmates from early childhood.

In 1979, I moved my family from Michigan to Texas, but the next year I flew back for the twenty-year class reunion. Because that bond of friendship was so unique, I never wanted to miss these LHS reunion gatherings.

My family next moved to Mesa, Arizona, in 1984 which was even further away, but going back to reunions was still something that was really important.

In 2002, the first time I retired, we would return to Michigan each summer to spend time with family. Because I always wanted to spend time with my LHS class of 1960 family, I let Marty Reynolds (chairman of the reunion committee) know when I was going to be there. He arranged a restaurant and got about twenty old friends together for what he called "Dinner with Dale."

The class celebrated "in-between" or "mini-reunions" when I would come to Grand Rapids.

These usually were held in September when I would visit with my family and friends.

For those of us who have faith in God and His promise of eternal life, there is great expectation that the relationships that we are nurturing here on earth will continue for all eternity. So as the classmates continue to say good-bye to each other in the months and years ahead, we believe that the good-byes are only temporary. We will soon be seeing each other again.

I can't help but think of Doug Greenwold, who was promoted to his heavenly home on June 23, 2019. For years I stayed connected with Doug through his ministry, Preserving Bible Times, and his work of providing resources for understanding Scripture in its cultural and historical context. Who better than Doug to give me a first tour of heaven?

Hope to see everyone at the next reunion whether here on earth or up above.

CHAPTER THIRTY-ONE

season of growth

Florida Park Bench Conversation (2022)

At our last park bench conversation of the season in Florida, Carol and I talked about how much we wanted to finish our book, but still plan to have park bench meetings and fun adventures after the book is published.

We miss the gals and are anxious to get home to our family of sisters. Carol had spoken with Sharon, and I spoke with Judy. They are looking forward to our return to Michigan.

We both were privileged to have our children and grandchildren visit us in Florida this year, plus my sister. A few Michigan friends met us for lunch.

Our park bench encounters this season included: Hammock Bay Pond (alligator sightings), Mackle Park (duck pond, dog park, and recreational facilities), Esplanade Marina (and mall), and two stops at Plummer Park, our oldest and dearest park bench stop.

It is at Plummer Park where we gave God the glory for Carol's stroke survival years ago. It was also in this same setting that we recently thanked the Lord for bringing healing to Carol this past winter.

As we sat on park benches, besides being grateful, we were hopeful to have our final friendship book edited and published. Our dream of writing a trilogy had been reduced to one book containing our lifelong journey. However, since I'm an eternal optimist, my counter was, "Maybe this book is complete, but only God knows what is coming next. Perhaps there will be a short story or a follow-up book in our future."

We giggled and said that Grandma Moses started painting at seventy-eight years of age and sold over sixteen hundred paintings, which are presently worth more than a million dollars apiece.

That ended our Grandma Moses conversation. The lesson was that the joy she received was the reason she painted. Carol and I agreed that the pure joy we have received while writing our friendship story has given us purpose. Our literary journey has given us fulfillment beyond our greatest expectations. Our purpose from the beginning has been to share with others our lifelong friendship journey, which has given us years of happiness.

If you are searching for purpose in your life, follow the two greatest commandments in God's Holy Word, which are to love the Lord your God with all that is within you, and love your neighbor as yourself.

Optimistically, Carol and I never doubted that the book would be completed in 2022. We are now almost a year later and are prayerful that the book will be published in 2023.

We discussed patience and that everything happens in God's time. We understood the pandemic slowed everything down; however, we are ready for action.

Lesson: It is worth waiting for the significant blessings bestowed on us by our loving Father.

Grand Haven Adventure (Summer 2022)

On our way to Grand Haven, Carol and I stopped in Spring Lake on a summer day in Michigan. We drove through the Grand Haven beach area. After passing the Eagle's Nest cottage where we stayed as teens, we felt inspired to drive to the local ice cream shop overlooking the channel.

Having parked the car, we walked to the small shop, ordered, and sat outside enjoying our treats. It was a déjà vu moment as we recalled doing the same thing many times in the past with the Draco Drips. Carol recollected walking to the shop for a treat and walking on the channel leading to the beach and shores of Lake Michigan.

Today we were short on time, so we rode around the familiar beach areas after we ate our ice cream. Many memories from the past resurfaced, mainly the excitement of being with the girls at the beach in our teen years.

Now, we both were embarking upon our eightieth birthdays in a few months. Could it be that we had been walking and driving in this area sixty-plus years ago as teenagers? We giggled as we reminisced about the carefree fun we enjoyed in the 1950s and early 60s.

"It would be fun to walk the channel with the Drips again," Carol said.

I agreed, however the practical side of our conversation convinced both of us that this would not happen. Our voices sounded encouraging, but our common sense dictated that very few of the women would be able to complete this task.

While driving back to Grand Rapids, Carol and I counted our blessings. We were still able to take day trips to have periodic adventures and travel to Florida during the cooler seasons in Michigan. When we parted, we knew our next group gathering would be to visit sister Sandy in Holland.

"Later, gator," I said as we hugged. I left Carol at Cook Valley Estates and headed home.

Redefining Octogenarians

The Draco friends had met one last time for lunch back in October of 2022, before Carol and I left for our seasonal stay in Florida. Hurricane Ian had recently hit southern Florida, and several locations suffered much devastation. The women were concerned, and discussed the wind and water damage that took place in Florida. We were sad to hear that 119 people perished during the storm.

The conversation switched to the fact that all of us had turned eighty years of age that year. We were now known as "octogenarians." Even though our generation is called "war babies" (WWII 1939-1945) and known as the "silent generation" (1925-1945), in many ways we are more like the "baby boomers' generation" (1946-1964). Most of us are computer literate, use smart phones, Google, order online, and own flat-screen TVs.

We no longer have landlines, overuse mayonnaise, or eat only at nationally known restaurants. NO SOCKS with our sandals!

We must admit we use cursive writing, but we dress well, still go to movies, enjoy a meal at an expensive restaurant, wine taste, and shop at gourmet shops and fashion boutiques. Travel is a luxury, and it's not always on senior cruises. Actually, we are pretty sophisticated for being senior citizens in the twenty-first century.

We talked about the many changes we have seen and experienced in our lifetime. It was unanimously agreed that our generation lived a charmed life in comparison with today's standards. Our parents and educators taught us to have good manners, to show respect, and to be honest. This was a way of life in the 1950s and early 1960s.

Children were taught to have high regard for others, no matter their age or status. This included family members, neighbors, classmates, school and church connections, community, and business acquaintances. Although there were disagreements, people were usually civil "back in the day." They would attentively listen to each other without animosity. There were two sides to the issue, and we would politely listen to both sides before making a decision. Physical confrontations and shootings were mostly acted out on television shows or in the movies at that time. We recall limited bullying or name-calling taking place when we were growing up.

Our music was the best. The artists introduced a new style of music in the 1950s called rock 'n' roll. Teenagers eagerly accepted this new rock 'n' roll music. The twist and creative dance steps also were popular. Elvis Presley became a household name, and record albums (now called vinyls) were selling out at the music stores. Rock 'n' roll stars appeared on television, performing in huge auditoriums and on outdoor stages all over the world.

God, Jesus, and gospel terms were acceptable in popular music. It was feel-good music with a positive message.

Society in the 1950s and Early 1960s

It was a different time in American culture. Most people believed in the value of God, family, and country. There was enormous pride in our American flag and in our national heritage. People respected veterans and those who served this country. The Pledge of Allegiance and the singing of "America" were common everyday occurrences in schools.

Students were encouraged to achieve in school, to do their best, to interact, and to help others succeed as well. Parents supported their children by attending school and church-related activities. All people were expected to work hard for a living. Personal responsibility and carrying out obligations were top priorities.

Was our generation perfect? NO! However, we were taught to respect others, their property, and their beliefs. The

Golden Rule of "Do unto others as you would have them do unto you" was a prevalent message. We watched our language, and in most cases, we were tolerant of different cultures and attitudes.

The media approach was less sensationalized, which put a more factual focus on the news, which was geared toward the positive.

The Power of Prayer

As mature senior women, we pray for our children, grandchildren, and great-grandchildren.

We pray for their safety and that they will make wise decisions.

We realize the power of prayer and understand that through the ages, God watches over and loves His children. He hears our prayers and intercedes for us.

As we age, our prayer lives become a more significant part of our daily routine. Talking with God brings us closer to Him. He is our Savior, and our friend. We cherish the time alone in His presence. Perhaps, the realization that He holds everything in the palms of His hands is more relatable to the mature believer.

CHAPTER THIRTY-TWO

our special relationship – january 2023

Connecting on a park bench has brought such delight to Carol and me over the past eighteen years. Although sitting on a park bench may not sound ultra-exciting in the twenty-first century, it is an adventure for two friends who have known each other their entire lives. Our park bench conversations bring joy, peace, fun, and security into a disconnected world.

Somehow, when we sit on a park bench marveling at God's beautiful creation, our minds are set on things above. The positive vibes rule out the negative things which are presently happening in today's world. We enjoy God's marvelous handiwork as we move around to different park benches in Michigan, our native home since birth, and in Florida, our retirement mecca.

The word "special" has many connotations. Carol and I decided that today we would sit on our favorite park bench and decide how to add the word "special" into our forever friendship story.

As we sat on our familiar swinging park bench, the sun shone on our chosen spot in Plummer Park on Marco Island.

It was peaceful and serene on this beautiful day in paradise as we reflected on our longtime friendship with our Draco sisters.

A few words used to describe our special group relationship include exceptional, favored, unique, and rare. The Bible doesn't use the word *special*. Instead, words such as beloved, precious, valued, and treasured are found in Scripture. However, Carol and I decided that one of the new topics included in our journey would be "special."

Motivation: He will lead us to the path of eternal righteousness, and into His everlasting arms.

Making Goals

Today as we sat on a park bench in Plummer Park, Carol was all aglow after recuperating from double pneumonia, which just months before had left her hospitalized three separate times. I truly marvel at how she survives, makes, and meets certain goals for resuming her activities, and gives God the glory. Instead of becoming bitter, Carol finds ways to stay active and involved in life while keeping an upbeat attitude, with a smile on her face.

As we sat on the park bench swinging, chatting, and laughing together, we decided that our main goal is to fully enjoy life for as long as we are able to move and breathe. Serving God and others fulfills our inner being and makes us happy and grateful.

Carol and I talked about our upcoming fall birthdays. I reminded her that we are still full of adventure; it matters not what age we are. Carol's funny little wide-eyed smile is something I have become accustomed to over the years, and my reply matched the look on both of our faces. I explained that we are full of adventure, even as the years roll by. We still have things to see and places to go.

Setting and Implementing Our Literary Goals

Today we are sitting on the same bench we had chosen almost eighteen years ago at this location in Plummer Park, which Carol had chosen and introduced me to. It gave me a feeling of déjà vu.

Other than having lighter hair now and a few more wrinkles, Carol appears as beautiful to me at this senior stage of her life as she always had. She has met her goals. She is alive, active, and has recently survived yet another crisis. Presently, she is doing well. Carol continues to say that God isn't ready to take her to her eternal home yet.

We both are still young at heart and able to move around.

As we were sitting on the park bench overlooking this lovely pond on Marco Island, everything seemed *special* on this day. God loves us. We have wonderful husbands, families who mean the world to us, a church where we are active members, and friends that bring us happiness. We are truly blessed.

Instead of pondering what the future years will bring, we live one day at a time. Our class has left a footprint in the Wyoming suburb of Grand Rapids. It is there that our memories of the past linger in our minds.

Many of our classmates are still actively driving and traveling places. We do admit that it makes sense to drive during the daylight hours, and we make more stops on motor trips.

Although it ultimately takes us longer to arrive at our destination, this doesn't make us feel decrepit or useless. Instead, it makes us feel happy to still be alive even though we don't move quite as swiftly as we once did.

Different Kinds of Grief

Although we have lost only two close Draco sisters, we have dealt with grief in many different types of circumstances. It is a natural response to mourn the loss of our departed loved ones.

Recently, I attended a grief class at our church after the loss of my sister, a brother-in-law, a cousin, and many close friends over a short period of time. These deaths seemed to keep happening and left me in various stages of mourning the dear ones who were called home.

Meeting with other members of the group who were grieving gave me comfort because being in a Christian community and sharing our feelings gives one hope for tomorrow. Some of the people were mourning loved ones who are in the process of dying. They too need to speak, listen to the sorrow that others feel, and express feelings from the depths of their hearts.

Each one of us deals with grief in a different way. Over time, we accept that our loved ones have departed. We have the blessed assurance in our hearts that we will be reunited in heaven with God and others. God promised that there will be no more sorrow, pain, or tears. That is comforting.

CHAPTER THIRTY-THREE

special

How Did the Word "Special" Come About?

Our sister, Donna, mentioned that her pastor preached a sermon on the fact that everyone is special in God's sight. I listened to that sermon online and continued to ponder long and hard about the word "special."

Our heavenly Father knows each one of us personally. He knows us by name and even the number of hairs on our head. For many of us, God will be the mainstay throughout our lives—from the time we were formed in the womb until He calls us home to live eternally with him.

Since our group is unique in our forever close relationship, we decided that focusing on how *special* we are to each other would be an excellent way to conclude our story.

Feeling "Special" – Donna Tillema

Donna stated that she feels *special* when she is entertaining her grandchildren. Getting them their favorite treats, doing various activities and projects with them gives her delight, plus the hugs that she gets from them are extra special. Her children thank her for being such a loving grandmother and great-grandmother.

It is important to Donna that her family faithfully follows God's pathway. She prays for her family and friends daily. The thing Donna especially loves about the Draco sisters is their relationship with God, especially when different opinions can be expressed and are always well-received.

> It takes time to process grief regarding a loved one's death, but we know that God is with us on this sad journey, and He will carry us through our sorrow.

Grief: When a death occurs, Donna feels that there is a strong, overwhelming feeling that never totally leaves the survivor. The departed person is not ever totally forgotten. Often you feel like you can give that person a call, and then it hurts all over again to realize that they are no longer available to speak with you. It takes time to process grief regarding a loved one's death, but we know that God is with us on this sad journey, and He will carry us through our sorrow.

My Faith Journey – Judy Walkotten

Judy's faith journey is special to her. She went as a child to Sunday school, catechism, and to both morning and evening Sunday services at 8th Reformed Church in Grand Rapids, Michigan.

As a teen, she attended Christian Endeavor (CE) and sang in the junior choir. Her family prayed before and after meals, and her father read the Bible after dinner. This gave her a good foundation to trust in the Lord.

Their four children were raised in the church and were baptized as infants. Later, they all made a public confession of faith at Fair Haven Reformed Church in Jenison, Michigan.

Judy stresses the importance of a positive and loving family environment, coupled with a God-centered personal church experience as necessary ingredients in raising children. She sees the results of this in her many grandchildren, and now her great-grandchildren's lives too.

Through Judy and Rich's years of marriage, she has always had trust and faith in the Lord Jesus Christ, and she will cling to His promises for the rest of her life.

Being "Special" – Sharon VandeGevel

Sharon feels that being *special* denotes that she has something better, more valuable, or worthy of bragging about, that few others have. That is certainly evident in the Draco Drips. She thinks that each member of the group has a personal gift, which means they could be or do anything they set their mind to do. They are kind, smart, generous, genuinely good, and positive thinkers. Every one of the sisters has had an issue that was life-changing, but Sharon thinks that every one of the sisters has managed the problems they were given with strength and courage.

My Faith Walk: There hasn't been a time that Sharon can remember when her parents didn't include their faith in whatever was happening throughout their lives. Their opinion was that you had to please God with all your actions. This included saying family prayers at dinnertime and individual prayers before going to bed. Also being always honest with your family and friends was an important virtue that her parents taught their children.

Everything was from God. Therefore, everything was viewed and judged by God. Although it didn't always make Sharon happy when she was a child, it certainly was good training for the years ahead.

Grief: To Sharon, grief is a very personal thing. People don't want to hang around a profoundly sad person, no matter how young or old the person may be. After her father died (when she was eleven and her little brother was seven), she became very introverted. Perhaps she could make her sadness disappear if she could hide it from people. Luckily, that didn't last long, because being the class clown was her forte, and she made the decision that being sad was not fun.

Sharon is thankful that her mother did her best to bring day-to-day living back to normal.

Although things were pretty grim at their home for far too long, Sharon unconsciously determined that this must change. Around that time, her fellow Draco Drip friend, Carol, told her that she would share her dad with Sharon. She didn't know what to say. She recalls being dumbfounded. But she also thought that it was the single, most "cool" thing a true friend could say!

After that, Sharon gave her sadness to the Lord and dealt with both the good and the bad in the best way she possibly could.

Senior Decisions: Based on the senior population, Sharon is not sure there are that many decisions to be made. However, one senior decision that her husband, Mel, and she made was to move into a senior living facility this past year. She admits that she is not in the best of health, and they wanted to make sure to have the continuum of care ready for the future. They preferred not to burden their children if they became terminally ill or move in with any of their children.

"Therein the problem lies because some ends seem to be more bitter than others," Sharon revealed. She went on to explain that if nothing else, Mel's goal was to make certain that at the end of their days, they leave a legacy of love for their family—a legacy of God the Father, Jesus the Son, and the Holy Spirit as a tribute. And for totally selfish reasons, they want their children to remember their parents with purely fond memories.

Sharon and Mel are starting to meet some wonderful people at Holland Home where they reside. It seems there are more women than men living there. She guesses that's common in retirement homes. It's a reminder that life goes on with or without your mate, and Sharon can count on the fact that this way, her husband can hang in there waiting for all the senior chicks to chase him down.

"Special" – Carol Jennings

When Carol hears the word "special," she thinks of the Draco sisters. They have been with her for as long as she can remember.

My Faith Journey: Carol's faith journey has lasted a long time. She first attended a church across the street from Lee K-12 School, in Grand Rapids, when she was a young student.

She walked to Burlingame Congregational Church where she attended various services and meetings. Upon turning sixteen years old, she would drive to church. It was later that she explored the Catholic church, which was also located in the neighborhood. This gave Carol the opportunity to compare the two religions.

> This journey has been a great ride for her. It has helped her to make good priorities in her life.

When Chuck and she married, they attended Westminster Presbyterian Church in Grand Rapids. This is the church where their three boys were active in Sunday school and in youth groups. Their son, Scott, and his wife, Susan, are still members and involved in this same church today.

Carol and Chuck moved to the shoreline in Grand Haven and became active members of the First Presbyterian Church for thirty years. In Florida for the winter months, they joined the United Church of Marco Island, where they presently remain involved in various capacities at their church.

Grief: Carol endured grief along with her journey of faith. This journey has been a great ride for her. It has helped her to make good priorities in her life. God has allowed her to experience a lifetime full of adventure from the beginning to whenever it will end.

After making multiple emergency trips to the Naples Community Hospital last year, Carol understands that God is in control of every situation, every day of her life. Although her journey has had several high and low periods, the Lord keeps giving her hope and strength for that appointed time when she meets her forever sisters in the halls of heaven.

Senior Decisions – Nancy Greenwold

These are some of the decisions that Nancy has personally made for her life as a senior.

Stay active and involved with family, friends, and church: Her parents were such good role models for her, by staying active. Her children still talk about how their grandparents rode on roller coaster rides with them when they were at Disney World. They were well into their sixties at that time. She thought about that as Doug and she went boogie boarding with their grandchildren in the Outer Banks when they were in their seventies.

Nancy's parents also drove to Hamilton, Michigan, or wherever the games were played when her brother, Rich, coached high school football. They brought a bushel of apples for the team every week. So, Nancy never misses a game or a performance for any of the grandchildren if she can help it. She always brings donuts to the swim team meets for the kids and their friends, which includes one additional donut for her.

Doug and Nancy were involved in various ways in whatever church they attended as the family moved around the country. It was the main source of their friendships, and they gained more than they ever gave in the form of friendships and spiritual growth.

Stay positive: Nobody enjoys listening to a complainer, and they don't need to hear the details of all your physical ailments. Nancy tries to keep it short when someone asks about her. Instead, she asks people about themselves rather than talking about herself all the time.

Take each day as a new opportunity to learn and grow: Live in the moment. Don't look back and think, *those days were better.* The "good old days" had tough times too. Today's world is more complicated, and we know so much more about what is going on everywhere, so we have additional awareness of the negative things taking place. But although Nancy gets discouraged and upset with things going on in the world, she tries to look for something good even in the difficult days. God often surprises her with something special. That is not a Pollyanna dream but a choice to focus on what she can do to make someone happy. She desires to live out her faith for the world to see.

Don't fight the changes you need to make as you age: Downsizing, moving, and giving up the things she can't do anymore—these are all difficult decisions to make. But they also bring new opportunities and friends into her life as well as less stress trying to keep up a lifestyle that is becoming more difficult to maintain.

For instance, Nancy's small condo has been a challenge for her to find room for everything she wants to keep. The good part is that she has made some new friends since she downsized, and it takes a lot less time to clean her smaller place. She no longer hosts the holidays since her kids have a lot more space than she has, and she doesn't miss it at all. Every stage of life has something good about it.

Trust in God: As we hear that more and more of our classmates are passing away, it can be frightening and make us anxious about our future. However, Nancy has found that God's timing is good. He gives us the strength that we need to get through the difficult times. She wants very much to show her children and grandchildren what it means to "die well," just as she has tried to show them what it means to "live well." She trusts God to be with her to the end.

Life is a gift, and Nancy has been blessed in so many ways. She truly tries to live a life of gratitude to God. She said, "I am grateful for the privilege of knowing that I am His."

CHAPTER THIRTY-FOUR

park bench conversations continue

Senior Secrets from Two Senior Ambassadors (February 2023)

On a beautiful morning in February, I picked Carol up at her condominium and we ran a few errands. We got ice cream on our way to find a park on Marco Island.

Our routine was reversed today. Usually, our park bench conversation comes first, then we treat ourselves to ice cream, but not today. When we parked close to Sweet Annie's, there was no decision to make. Our ice cream high came first, and then Carol and I went to a park.

Upon finding a swinging park bench in Veterans' Community Park, we asked a young man to take a photograph of us sitting on the bench. He willingly agreed to do so.

Our first topic of conversation was regarding Carol and me being recently referred to as "senior ambassadors." We laughed and decided that perhaps we have some senior secrets to share as gems of wisdom with anyone who cares to read or listen.

Our last Florida park bench conversation
– Veterans' Community Park – 2023

Could we be ambassadors because we have a positive outlook on life and endeavor to be upbeat and happy? If so, we humbly accept this most generous title, and we'll try to impart some helpful pearls of wisdom to others.

Yet Another Decade Has Passed

Swinging on the park bench, Carol and I recalled starting to write our lifetime story when we had both just retired and were in our early sixties. We had never thought for a moment about decades passing so quickly. Our decision was to forever be sprightly seniors who would enjoy each day of life.

With that kind of attitude, Carol and I pass on to you what is in our hearts, even though each new day is now an added blessing and seems a bit dearer as each year and decade passes.

Motivation: We focus on the good, the light, and the mountaintops instead of the bad, the darkness, and the low valleys of life.

We feel blessed to be sitting on a park bench enjoying the sunlight, the birds, the flowers, and the view of the pond in front of us. We know that God created the entire world, even the birds and flowers of the field, and He takes care of them, feeds them, and nurtures them. We know that He is in control of everything. The sunshine and pond were added benefits that day, as well as the swing that we were sharing and especially the power of friendship which surrounds us on these adventures.

Are we always positive, upbeat, and eternally happy? NO. We are human. We understand reality, but we also choose to focus on living each day to the best of our ability. We know that we can't do everything on our own. We need to invite God to help us through prayer to constantly love, care, support, protect, and forgive us.

Death of a Second Draco Sister

Speaking of reality, Carol and I discussed the startling text that had arrived a few days earlier on Valentine's Day. Hospice had notified the family a few months earlier that our dear Draco sister, Sandy, would soon be called to her heavenly home.

When it happened, the Draco women were still saddened by the starkness of reality. Most of the sisters were in Grand Rapids and attended the funeral service for Sandy. Nancy lives in Maryland, and Carol and I were in Florida, which made it impossible to fly home for the service. In fact, Michigan was in the middle of an ice storm, and some of the local airports were closed.

Many phone calls, texts, and emails kept us updated, and we were sent the memoriam information with Sandy's photo.

As we continued to swing, we recalled the last time we had seen Sandy along with the Lee School women who had attended kindergarten with her—Carol, Judy, Sharon, Sue, and me. We had met in the memory unit of the care home where Sandy had resided for the past seven years. August was her birthday month, and we spent time with Sandy and her daughter, Susan.

Susan had met us in August for Sandy's birthday for several years, where we presented her mother with cards and hugs. Susan had her mother adorned in a new outfit with her hair and nails done. Sandy seemed to know it was a special occasion, and she always smiled.

This final year, we met Bob, Sandy's husband, and the other Draco sisters, Barb, Donna, and Jackie for lunch at a restaurant. They were unable to join us at the home, but we took a group picture after we ate.

Sandy interested in *The Promised Piece*

A Memory to Cherish

Five years earlier, Susan had sent us a photo of her mother reading *The Promised Piece*, the first book Carol and I wrote about our forever friendship relationship with the Draco women.

Upon presenting Sandy with a copy of the book when we visited, Susan later read the story to her mother. They were distracted, but Sandy continued looking at the book and the pictures of the past, appearing very interested.

Just days before Sandy passed away, this particular picture of Sandy (from five years ago) appeared on my internet screen. I sent the picture to Susan and to our classmates. A few days later Sandy passed away. It touched my heart that Susan wrote, "Thank you so much for writing this book and sharing the wonderful Draco Drip memories with everyone."

What gives Sandy's sisters confidence and encouragement is that she had been a Christian daughter, sister, wife, mother, grandmother, aunt, and friend to many. We know beyond a shadow of a doubt that we will be reunited with her and Marcia and all our departed loved ones someday.

The thought gave Carol and me a memory to cherish as we sat on the park bench swinging and thinking of Sandy and Marcia. They were blood cousins who are now free from all of life's burdens; plus they are reunited. We picture them waiting for the rest of their beloved Draco sisters to join them someday.

Independent Facility Living Adjustments

Carol and Chuck led the way to living in an independent home in Cook Valley, a Grand Rapids facility. Although Carol initially had a difficult transition, she now enjoys the people and the activities available to them. She advocates for Cook Valley and feels safe and secure at this facility.

Many of the couples in our group started looking at various places in the suburbs near to where their families live. In fact, Donna and Arn moved to The Oaks at Byron Center, an independent living home, and Sharon and Mel followed by moving to Holland Home in Breton Woods. Jackie, who is now a widow, moved to a Wayland care facility. All the decisions have been good ones, because they each researched and found what suited their needs best, in an area where they are comfortable.

A few other couples have put their names on waiting lists at various facilities and have decided where they want to live when the time is right for them to move.

Life and Legacy Planning with Grown Children

For years, Carol and I have discussed making our pre-planned wishes and to effectively communicate them to our adult children when the time is right. Today, we were more in the mood to talk about our plans and wishes and about having this very serious discussion with our children, especially since our dear sister had passed away days earlier.

The Jennings were ahead of us in the pre-planning process. I listened closely as Carol explained how after much research and organization, Chuck had gotten all their information together. He has also provided several yearly letters to their family members, keeping them well-informed of Carol's and his desires.

It is recommended by estate planners to hire the services of an attorney who specializes in estate and financial planning. Some people look at their estates as being a detailed legacy for their children, and others have less complicated financial and estate plans. However, it is helpful for survivors to have funeral pre-planned arrangements, durable power of attorney, a living will, and last will and testament documents, etc., in place. Once the documents are completed, they should be kept in a safe place known by the executor.

Being able to communicate a written or verbal plan with adult children is the beginning of a smooth transition process before the death of a parent. If one parent is still living, their care and needs must be clearly documented.

What is important to us is the close family bond that we pray will stay in place after our deaths. The Christian values, the traditions, and the stories will remain from generation to generation to keep the legacy of our family alive.

A Call to Our Agent

Upon leaving the park bench, Carol and I sat in the car and had a conference call with Diane, our literary agent. She had spoken to the publishing company and they were ready to edit our manuscript.

We told her that we had completed our final park bench topics and would be submitting the manuscript to her. All three of us were ready to proceed to get the book edited, and we were eager to read our story after the final edit.

Although every good thing goes through a process before completion, having others excited about our journey makes us happy and prayerful that we soon will have a copy of *The Power of Friendship* in our hands.

Many people have been praying for the completion of our forever friendship book. Our pastors, our families, and our friends are eager to join us by reading about our journey.

Motivation: It is the grace of God that has given us several decades together.

Florida Adventure 2023

It was exciting that Carol and I could enjoy a full day of adventure again. Carol picked me up for a day of fun and enjoyment on Marco Island, Florida. Other than having our usual park bench conversations and mini-adventures this season, we had a diverse day of activities to look forward to today.

We started out at the Wesley Park Methodist Church to hear an author book review. Next, we drove to our local United Church for the final Mending Hearts Grief Group meeting and luncheon of the season. Since Carol and I had lost our Draco friend, Sandy, the month before, this meeting was a comfort to people who had shared losses of family and friends.

Shopping was next. Carol bought some cosmetics while I found a blouse in the perfect lavender shade at Kay's On The Beach. After shopping, we happened to be near our favorite ice cream shop, so we decided to stop and splurge on a new flavor today.

As we approached the door, an elderly gentleman held it open for us. We engaged in conversation, and he shared that he had just lost his wife. We continued to talk with him, bought him ice cream, and he sat with us. He was almost ninety years old and appeared lonely but was a friendly man.

Finally, we drove to the Marco Movies and saw *Jesus Revolution*, a newly released Christian film about the Jesus movement in the 1970s.

It was eight o'clock in the evening when I arrived home from an active, adventurous day. Art had arrived home from a Detroit Tiger exhibition baseball game in Lakeland, Florida, where he met his nephew. We had a late dinner, and I took a well-deserved bubble bath and read.

Before retiring for the evening, I sent a message to Carol about some free dates next week. The four of us planned to go to dinner. It is with gratefulness in my heart that I thank the Lord for a day spent with my forever friend.

Lee K-12 School Celebrates Their Hundredth Anniversary

Lee K-12 School was built and opened in 1923. In September 2023, all Lee High School Alumni are invited to a hundredth anniversary open house at the school. Our class of 1960 will be represented at the event, and this includes the Draco Drips and many classmates. Alumni from various classes will represent former graduates, both local and those who attend the event from other states.

Two of my biological sisters graduated from Lee School, and the three of us will attend this event. Sadly, one sister and all of our aunts who graduated from this school are now deceased. My father also attended Godfrey-Lee School. Dad would have turned 105 years old this May.

There are family and friend connections which are sure to bring laughter and tears at this joyous hundredth commemorative centennial celebration.

Invitation to the LHS Hundredth Anniversary, 2023 (postcard)

CHAPTER THIRTY-FIVE

spiritual reflections

The Season of Easter

When growing up, Easter meant the Easter Bunny brought baskets full of candy and left them on the table early Easter morning. Then the family would dress in their Sunday best and go to church to praise God because Jesus had risen. He had risen indeed!

In our middle and high school years, Easter was reflected on Ash Wednesday, Palm Sunday, Maundy Thursday, Good Friday, and with the resurrection of Jesus on Easter Sunday morning.

Now, as retirees, we look forward to all these services at church and enjoy the fellowship of other believers who understand the significance of Jesus' death, burial, and resurrection.

Hallelujah! Jesus was resurrected from the grave three days later, He ascended into heaven, and He sits on the right hand of God the Father Almighty!

The important thing is that our risen Savior lives and reigns forever in our hearts.

Our pastor stated so eloquently how the number three is representative of many biblical facts.

Reflections from Rev. Dr. Mark Williams

When challenges come to the final years of our lives on earth—and there are many challenges related to aging and growing older—we remind ourselves that God will deliver us. God will deliver us through all adversity, including death.

> Easter was the day that pain and darkness got swallowed up in victory!

As we age, we resonate with the Easter story. Easter is a three-day story.

Good Friday was the first day of the story. Those in power arrested Jesus, lashed Him with a whip, pierced Him with a sword, and hung Him on a cross. Like Christ, we know physical pain. We know the pain of a hard diagnosis, of a bad back, of fading eyesight, of cognitive decline, not to mention slips and falls. We know pain.

Holy Saturday was the second day of the story. Pontius Pilate posted a guard to stand watch over the tomb. The tomb was dark. Like Christ, we know darkness. We know the darkness of grief and the darkness of feeling alone at times in our final years of life on earth.

Rev. Dr. Mark Williams

Easter, however, was the third day of the story. Easter was God's Day. On Easter, resurrection happened. Easter was the day that pain and darkness got swallowed up in victory!

Easter is just one of a series of three-day stories in the Bible that involves crisis and urgency. When in prison, Joseph said to his fellow prisoners: "Within three days, you will be set free." When the Israelite people arrived at Sinai, God said: "Be ready on the third day, because on that day the Lord will come down on Mount Sinai in the sight of all the people." When Joshua and his people feared entry into the Promised Land, God said to them: "Be strong and courageous, for three days from now you will take possession of the land."

When Israel was threatened with genocide, Queen Esther said that she would fast for three days and then go to the king to seek deliverance for her people. When Abraham was called by God to sacrifice Isaac, Abraham went on a three-day journey to the altar. Want to guess how long Jonah was in the belly of the big fish? Jonah was there three days before being released. In Scripture, three-day stories are stories of deliverance. Right now, a situation may not be good in our lives. Right now, despair, regrets, and disappointment might fill our hearts. But a better day is coming. Why?

Because Our God Is the God of the Third Day!

Indeed, as we age, many of us find ourselves living in a "first day" and "second day" world—a world that at times can be as painful as crucifixion and as dark as a tomb. We live in a world that is isolated and fearful, a world where disease and war have devastated many. We struggle to come to terms with it all. Simply put, we live in a world full of heartache—a first- and second-day world for sure!

Nevertheless, we have reason to hope even in our old age. We have reason to be encouraged. We have reason to believe in the mission and ministry of Christ and the church. We have reason to believe that a better day is coming. Why?

Because we worship a third-day God!

"For I delivered to you as of first importance what I also received: that Christ died for our sins in accordance with the Scriptures, that he was buried, that he was raised on the third day in accordance with the Scriptures, and that he appeared to Cephas, then to the twelve" (1 Cor. 15:3–5 ESV).

293

Reflections from Pastor Dale Kronemeyer

About sixty-six years ago, many of us memorized part of "The Raven" by Edgar Allan Poe. In this poem, the narrator asked many questions of the Raven, who is called "thing of evil." Two questions were: "Is there a balm in Gilead?" and "Would his soul ever 'clasp' his radiant Lenore again in the afterlife?"

As in many of his previous responses, the Raven again replied, "Nevermore."

This poem reflected the darkness and the hopelessness that flowed from the life of the author himself.

As I pondered about how much brighter our lives were, I considered the things that shaped my life in those early years: (1) wonderful parents who loved me and guided me in a walk of faith; (2) good teachers who gave me a hunger for learning; (3) a band director who inspired and taught me to be the best baritone horn player that I could be and who also amazed

us when eighty-plus people brought their different instruments and skills together with hard work to make beautiful music and win awards; (4) sports that taught each of us the value of teamwork and maintaining a good attitude whether we won or lost; and for me, (5) the YFC Club that challenged me in the area of leadership when I became

Pastor and classmate, Dale Kronemeyer

president of the organization. Through all the school experiences, we developed friendships that have lasted a lifetime and memories that still bring a smile.

As the old classic song sung by Bob Hope says, "Thanks for the memories."

Most of the members of the Lee High School class of 1960 who are still here, will celebrate their eighty-first birthdays in 2023. We all are aware that most of this life is now behind us. But we move forward knowing that we have been abundantly blessed. We cherish the memories of the past as we continue to make a few more in the few short years we have left.

Along with joy, there are also seasons of sorrow and grief as we say our good-byes, but unlike the message of "The Raven," we find hope even in our grief. As the writer of 1 Thessalonians says, "We do not grieve like the rest of mankind who have no hope." Through our faith in God through Jesus Christ, I believe that we all can face life and death with the comfort and assurance that God will guide our paths, and someday soon He will bring us to our eternal home where we will see our "Lenores" again. As the psalmist said, "Even though I walk through the valley of the shadow of death, I will fear no evil, for you are with me," and closes out the Twenty-Third Psalm (NIV) with "and I will dwell in the house of the Lord forever."

> We cherish the memories of the past as we continue to make a few more in the few short years we have left.

But for now, I believe that as long as we have breath, we have a purpose. We can still stand against the influence of the Ravens of this world with their "nevermore" attitudes by living and sharing a life of hope and faith.

about the authors

MARILYN LUTKE EMERY is a joyful octogenarian, whose main goal in life is to spread God's love. Education is of utmost importance to Marilyn, who obtained her undergraduate degree in Speech/Communications and English, and her three master's degrees in educational administration, Gifted and Talented Education, and K-12 Reading Language Arts. After teaching and consulting for several years, Marilyn wrote language arts curriculum, presented educational in-service programs, and taught college English classes.

In her retirement, Marilyn is very active in her church. She recently served as president of Women's Fellowship of United Church of Marco Island. Concurrently, she was a member of the Church Life and Growth Committee. She is also a liturgist and greeter.

She and her husband, Art, split their time between Michigan and Florida. They enjoy traveling worldwide, entertaining, visiting their family, and spending time at their summer home in northern Michigan. Marilyn is very happy to share her heartfelt story of how her lifetime friends have enriched her life, including her besties, the "Draco Girls," for over seven decades. Her forever friend, Carol, was the inspiration for her book. With five children, fifteen grandchildren, and one great-grandchild, Marilyn feels truly blessed.

Marilyn was born and raised in Grand Rapids, Michigan, along with three sisters and her brother.

CAROL FORD JENNINGS was raised in Grand Rapids, Michigan, as an only child. She met Marilyn when she was five years old, and both attended K-12 in the community.

A well-rounded student, Carol was involved in many

school activities, including the Future Teachers of America, the Girls Athletic Association, Pep Club, and the school choir.

Carol studied at the local community college, worked at a bank where she met her husband, Chuck, and then completed her degree, majoring in business and minoring in literature— all while raising three sons. Carol worked part-time at a bookstore for ten years, assisting customers, and using her literature expertise. She is a longtime member of Philanthropic Educational Organization (P.E.O.).

Carol and Chuck enjoy worldwide travel. Memorable trips include China, South America, and a global WWII trip that started in Hawaii.

Now retired, Carol and Chuck spend most of their time at their condo in Florida and enjoy summers in Grand Rapids, Michigan, where Carol spends time with her family, including eight grandchildren and one great-grandchild—and the Draco girls!

acknowledgments

Carol and I are thankful that we were able to continue our journey with suggestions from Diane Jones, our literary agent, who encouraged us to extend our book. Her ideas and guidance have been greatly valued throughout the years.

The caring and ongoing interest in this project from our families and friends have inspired us to continue writing and moving forward.

We are grateful to our forever Draco friends for their written contributions. The friendships we have shared over the years, and the joy they have given us on our journey, could never be replaced.

Our deepest appreciation goes to all our additional friends from Lee High School, and to our acquaintances, for showing an interest in our projects. They have truly been an inspiration to us during the years.

Other family members who contributed time and helpful suggestions were Tara and Nick Kacher, Tiffany Twa, and Dean and Parker Amick who assisted with technology. My sisters, Joanie and Marcia, always had listening ears, and multiple friends inquired regularly about the progress of the book.

All praise to God for directing me to write our lifelong story, and for blessing Carol, our Draco sisters, and our pastors as we worked on this special project. He led us on this inspirational pathway of sharing our story of friendship … for which we are thankful to Him.

discussion questions

Chapters 1–5

- Have you ever gone more than the extra mile to help a friend in serious need?
- How do you compare your school years with friends and family to that of Marilyn and Carol?
- What are some of your favorite memories of childhood and youth?
- Do you have lifelong friends? If so, how often do you keep in touch with them?
- What can you learn from people who are disciplined to journal for decades?
- Did you stay in touch with your high school friends or go your own separate ways?
- Do you know anyone who had to recover from a major medical crisis? How did they handle the situation? Did they fight to regain what they lost, or were they discouraged and tempted to give up?
- Marilyn and Carol believe in paying it forward—helping others who suffered like they did. Have you done something similar? Why do you think it is helpful?

Chapters 6–10

- Do you attend class reunions? What is your favorite story from one of your reunions?
- Marilyn and Carol enjoyed sitting on park benches for their visits. Do you have a favorite place to meet with friends?
- Carol explains how the stroke caused her to think differently: "God was in my life before, but now He is in charge of my life." How do you relate to this statement of faith?
- In chapter seven, Marilyn and Carol talk about the "rhythm of life." Read this section in your group. Do you see the rhythm that Marilyn describes? Would you be willing to share difficult aspects of your own life if it would help others?
- Have you had to accept the responsibility of being the caretaker for a loved one? What did you learn from the experience?
- After reading about Grand Rapids, Michigan, if you had to describe your home state, what points of interest would you highlight when describing it?
- What is your favorite girlfriend story?
- Imagine a time when women had no support systems for miscarriages and stillborn babies. How do you think women managed their anguish?

Chapters 11–15

- How does your faith help you with the death of a loved one?
- Did you struggle with maintaining your faith during a very difficult time?
- What are some of the joys and challenges of adult dating and second marriages?
- Have you lost any of your close friends? Share the experience.

- What might it feel like to receive a death sentence from a doctor when you feel normal?
- Pastor Dale Kronemeyer marvels at the lifelong friendships in his class. Why did their closeness last so long?
- Doug mentions that their class was blessed but didn't know it. What might we take for granted in our younger years, and why?
- Does the family life in the 1950s and 60s mentioned at the end of chapter fifteen sound familiar or different than your recollections?

Chapters 16–20

- Have you returned to your hometown and found that it had changed dramatically?
- Explain what changes you observed.
- Discuss the importance of having purpose in your senior years.
- Why do some seniors describe themselves as "young at heart?"
- Marilyn and Carol reinvented themselves in their senior years. What did this mean to them? How do you relate? How can you prepare for what might be coming in the future?
- Do you have a senior moment you can share with your group, or have you witnessed a humorous senior moment?
- How can you continue to be a good friend to your close friend who has been diagnosed with Alzheimer's?
- What did you learn about how Marilyn and Carol choose to spend their time? Would you change the way you spend yours?
- Marilyn and Carol spoke about raising their children in the faith. Do you have any hopes or expectations of your children?

Chapters 21–25

- If you could speak to anyone, living or dead, who would it be?
- Marilyn and Carol remarked about how amazing it is that after all these years, the Draco girls are still learning things about each other. You think you know someone, and then discover something new about them. Have you been surprised to learn something new about a longtime friend or family member? Can you share your experience?
- What is your favorite birthday memory?
- Discuss how COVID restrictions affected seniors. Was it different than other age groups?
- One of the subtitles in chapter twenty-three is called, "Is Different Good?" as it relates to navigating COVID. What did the authors say about attitude? Do you agree?
- What was your takeaway from the firsthand 9/11 and JFK assassination accounts and how the Draco friends feel about tragic events in history?
- How did Marilyn and Carol feel about the loss of their Draco friend's spouse and the limitations to support his widow during 2020?
- How did COVID directly affect your family or friends?

Chapters 26–30

- Words of affirmation are important. At Carol and Chuck's golden wedding anniversary, Carol gave a speech and offered encouragement and spoke of her love for each individual member of her family. If you have done something similar, how did it impact your family?
- How would this book have been different if it had been written twenty years ago?
- Is there a friend from the past whom you are tempted to reconnect with? Do you plan to contact them? If not, what's stopping you?

- Marilyn and her sisters are grateful for one another. This isn't the case in every family. What are ways to improve these relationships?
- Why do seniors reflect and wonder how quickly their lives have passed?
- Carol encourages seniors in chapter twenty-nine to look at life through the lens of truthfulness and accept that we are included in the golden generation, the "venerable" who are revered and respected at this advanced stage of life. How does it benefit seniors to accept this stage of life?
- In chapter thirty, Dale Kronemeyer said, "I wonder often how much more time I have on this earth and wonder how my death will happen.... I carry with me the glorious promise that our heavenly home is a place where there will be no more sorrow, sickness, or pain." Do you ever wonder how you will die one day? How does "the glorious promise" help you as you contemplate your future?
- What kind of research do you think the author had to do to write this book?

Chapters 31–35

- In chapter thirty-one, the authors talk about "redefining octogenarians." Are you a typical senior or have you in some way redefined the stereotype of a senior lifestyle?
- At the end of chapter thirty-one, the authors talk about the power of prayer. Read this short section in your group. How has prayer helped you?
- How do the authors acknowledge their senior limitations? How has your life become more limited and what are you doing to stay active to the best of your ability?
- How do you deal with grief, especially major or multiple events?
- What picture or illustration did you find especially interesting, and explain why?

- In chapter thirty-four, the "senior ambassadors" impart their philosophy. What will you take away from this story and these women?
- Pastor Mark Williams talks about the God of the third day—the God of the resurrection. Day one and day two may be filled with heartache and disappointment, but on the third day everything changes. One day, our lives will come to an end. How does keeping our eyes on the hope of the resurrection help us, especially in the senior stage of life?
- What's your overall impression of this book?

please help us reach more readers!

D ear Friends,

     Carol and I hope you enjoyed *The Power of Friendship* as much as we enjoyed writing it. If you were inspired by the book, we invite you to ask your friends and relatives to read it as well.

     Here are a few ways that you can help us spread the word:

- Recommend the book to friends – word-of-mouth is still the most effective form of advertising.
- Purchase additional copies to give away as gifts on my website.
- Post a 5-Star review on Amazon.
- Write about the book on your Facebook, Twitter, Instagram, LinkedIn—any social media you use!
- If you blog, consider referencing the book, or publishing an excerpt from the book with a link back to my website. You have my permission to do this if you provide proper credit and backlinks.

The best way to connect is by visiting
www.MarilynMEmery.com